To
Sheila
With my very Best

Pat

Patrick Church has devoted his entire life to the world of cinema. From the 60s, through to the present day his passion, commitment and determination has never faltered. His first book, *The Smallest Show on Earth* is a detailed autobiography of his life in cinema which gained him the name "Mr Movie Man", an apt title no one can deny. With that old saying "leave them wanting more", he has finally succumbed to the many requests to tell more of his endeavours in steering a small-town cinema to the success it is today.

To my son, Stuart, whose invaluable assistance in editing and research help made this book a reality.

To my wife, Geraldine, who has unreservedly supported my every whim throughout the past 55 years of cinema management.

To all my friends and colleagues, without them there were times I may have well thrown in the towel, but their encouragement always spurred me on "failure was not an option".

Patrick Church

MR MOVIE MAN

AUSTIN MACAULEY PUBLISHERS™

LONDON ∗ CAMBRIDGE ∗ NEW YORK ∗ SHARJAH

Copyright © Patrick Church 2022

The right of Patrick Church to be identified as author of this work has been asserted by the author in accordance with sections 77 and 78 of the Copyright, Designs and Patents Act 1988.

All rights reserved. No part of this publication may be reproduced, stored in a retrieval system, or transmitted in any form or by any means, electronic, mechanical, photocopying, recording, or otherwise, without the prior permission of the publishers.

Any person who commits any unauthorised act in relation to this publication may be liable to criminal prosecution and civil claims for damages.

All of the events in this memoir are true to the best of author's memory. The views expressed in this memoir are solely those of the author.

A CIP catalogue record for this title is available from the British Library.

ISBN 9781398407381 (Paperback)
ISBN 9781398415539 (Hardback)
ISBN 9781398407404 (ePub e-book)

www.austinmacauley.com

First Published 2022
Austin Macauley Publishers Ltd®
1 Canada Square
Canary Wharf
London
E14 5AA

Cast

I would like to express special thanks for the courtesy of the BURY FREE PRESS in allowing me to include past press clippings.

I would also like to thank everyone that supported me from media, staff and friends. I Couldn't have done it without you.

With kind permission of:

Bury mercury
East Anglian daily times
Barry Peters
Graham Turner
Paul Derrick
Su Anderson
Phil Morley
Jo Thewlis
Will Jefford
Lyn Goleby
Chris Peters
Jo Edgeley
Bernard Wright
and many more.

Prologue

I would like to start this collection of memories with a mention of Mum and Dad, because, without them, my life and this story would never be.

Dad

Dad was born in Peterborough in 1923. He was called up for National Service in 1942 and it was during this period that he got stationed at Newark, Nottinghamshire where he met and fell in love with Patricia Christie. After a whirlwind romance they married and lived for a short while in Peterborough. It was not a very happy start to their marriage as Dad's leave was soon over and he had to return to base which left Mum a little bewildered and lonely in what seemed to her to be an alien place. Being a country lass, she was just not used to being in a large city environment and despite Dad's family members trying to be nice to her, it was so different from that small cottage in the village of Elston, near Newark-on-Trent.

Two children soon followed (me being one of them), but that feeling of isolation never went away. Then suddenly with the demise of her foster parents the opportunity arose for them to move back into that cottage in Elston whilst Dad completed his National Service.

Once demobbed, Dad found it very difficult to find employment and it was his turn to feel isolated from his city roots, but 'love prevails' and his certainly did. He had the love of a good wife and children as they came along.

In later years when their children were grown up and married themselves, they would take it in turns to visit each of us and often stay over. We, as a young and upcoming family, so looked forward to their visits as they were always full of enthusiasm and interest in all we were doing.

I fondly remember the times that I took Dad to the Bury St Edmunds cattle market, just the two of us. He loved being there listening to the farmers with their many different dialects, sitting at the refreshment stall with his giant mug of tea. What laughs we had and he always came home with trays of fruit and vegetables he had bartered for—so triumphant, telling us all at home just how he had got them.

Poor old Dad was taken from us at the age of 63 after suffering for some time with that dreaded disease, cancer, but the love he instilled, got us all through this terrible ordeal and with so many fond memories of years past that it never felt he ever really left us.

Mum

Born Patricia Eileen Christie on 17 November 1925 in Newark, Nottinghamshire, Mum was fostered from the age of six months. She grew up wondering about why she had been abandoned by her natural parents. These thoughts would always remain with her. She had quite a strict "Victorian" style upbringing but was loved and well cared for. Mum met, then married our father, Fred, on 9 December 1944. They had six children plus our sister Wendy, who was still born.

In the early years she worked incredibly hard to keep all of us kids with limited resources, but we all remember the fun times we had, playing cricket and rounders with her. We also played silly card games and she would tickle us until we just could not take it anymore. She had her very own way of calling us from our different play areas. It was a special-sounding whistle that we mimicked to the words 'we are fish'. This sound would echo across the fields and only we would know just what it meant. Looking back now, I suppose it could be attributed to being like a sheepdog rounding up her flock.

Mum also had these many little sayings that have stayed with me throughout my life. To give you some idea:

What's for dinner? "Shim shams for lame ducks."

How old are you, Mum? "As old as my tongue and a little older than my teeth."

And there was many a day she was:

"Going to have our guts for garters." Oh, the memories.

During her later years and after extensive research by our brother Alan, she became re-united with her previously unknown blood relations in Canada: something she cherished most dearly and she made two visits to meet them all.

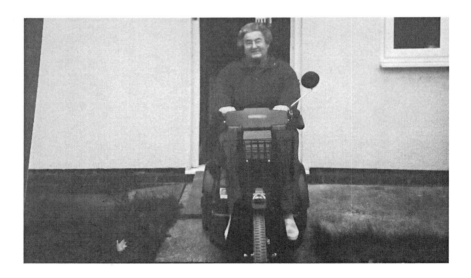

Her many friends in Ramsey will no doubt remember her zipping around on her mobility buggy (one of the best things we ever did for her). Oh, the laughs it created, good job it was racing green.

For our mum, family was her everything and her love shone on them all. Dad and their six children plus all the daughters and sons-in-law and grandchildren, as they came along and grew up, followed by her great grandchildren. As she lay in that hospital bed, her final words were: "Night Night", as she peacefully passed away to meet her Fred. I even have a tear in my eye writing this.

My story revolves around cinema. It still is and always has been, my life. This book is about all of the cinemas I have been involved with, for whatever reason. I have spent 54 years of my life at the Abbeygate Cinema in Bury St Edmunds, so this is the main topic of my life. During these years the cinema has seen ten different ownerships, each one bringing their own different challenges, and it is very akin to having had ten different jobs over that period.

It is worth mentioning that for anyone who has read my first book, *The Smallest Show on Earth*, some of the tales within this book are an embellishment of incidents previously documented. For those that have not had the pleasure, it may be worthwhile to check it out for a better understanding.

Chapter One

I was born in Peterborough in 1947. At that time, Peterborough boasted six cinemas on which I shall elaborate later.

My early years were spent in the small village of Elston, just a few miles outside Newark-on-Trent, Nottinghamshire. This is where I would have my first ever cinema experience.

It was at the Savoy Cinema that I was first introduced to the magic and wonder of the movies. Being a lad of just five years old, The Savoy had an immediate impact on me and even at this young age my future seemed to be mapped out.

Because I was so very young at the time, my recollection of this cinema is very sketchy, but I remember that it made such an impression on me as being something so very different to anything I had experienced before and I was completely mesmerised by it all. It wasn't until years later I felt compelled to do some research on the venture and was intrigued to learn the following information.

The Savoy

Sixty-eight years after my visit, my research revealed that it had opened on 30 January 1936 with Irene Dunne in *Roberta*. It had a rather narrow entrance on middle gate, with most of the facade made up of windows. The foyer walls were lined in mahogany panels. Inside the auditorium, seating was provided in stalls and circle levels. I vividly remember seeing two films here, and they made such an impact on me and my imagination that I strongly believe that this is what set me on the path of spending the rest of my life being cinema-minded.

Initially it was independently operated. But in the early 1950s, it was taken over by the Leeds-based, Star Cinemas chain (now isn't that a coincidence as I would be working for them in my later years). The single-screen Savoy Cinema was closed on 15 April 1972 and was converted into a four-screen cinema. It was re-opened as Studios 1-2-3-4 on 22 June 1972. All four auditoriums were in the former stalls area. The studios operated until closing on 10 May 1984 when the building was sold for redevelopment. Today it is in use as a branch of the Halifax Building Society.

Chapter Two

Very soon after my early visits to The Savoy, the family moved out of Elston and relocated in the Fenland district, in the small rural town of Ramsey, near Huntingdon.

Ramsey had a cinema, The Grand, and although I never made a visit until much later in my life, I would look at it from the outside in wonderment every time we went past.

After being in Ramsey for several years I consented to move away from the family to live with my grandparents so as to be company for my very nervous grandmother. This meant going back to Peterborough, in the New England area, a suburb of the city.

As I indicated earlier, Peterborough had no fewer than 6 cinemas in operation during this time and for a boy like me who was fascinated with cinema and the movie business, this was like Heaven on Earth.

The City Cinema

Upon entering the city, looking out from the front of a double-decker bus (the normal way to travel in the 1950s), the very first view, for me anyway, as I came across the bridge over the River Nene was the City Cinema.

The only film I remember seeing there before its closure in 1960 was *Soloman & Sheba* and I think it was my one and only visit to this cinema. It was demolished in the summer of 1961, and an extension to the adjacent Woolworths store was built on the site. It later became a branch of Marks & Spencer.

I was so impressed by the sheer scale of the building; I questioned my Uncle John on its history and found out that the City Cinema had been operating since 1927 with seating available in circle and stalls.

In 1937 the Bancroft family took over the site and operated under the title of 'Peterborough Amusements'.

Over many following years, whenever I heard the name 'Jack Bancroft', the City Cinema always came back to mind.

Further down the main street the next cinema to come into view was…

The Broadway

The Broadway Theatre, Peterborough was originally built for Odeon Theatres Ltd, as a single-screen cinema with seating for 1,752 people. The cinema opened on the 2nd of September 1937 with the film *Theodora Goes Wild*.

I was a regular visitor to this cinema and watched many films there. In later times I was invited to their projection room where I learnt the history behind the façade; in fact, after a while one could always find me in their projection room as I was totally fascinated with the latest film projectors, the Kalee 21. They have always been my favourite projector.

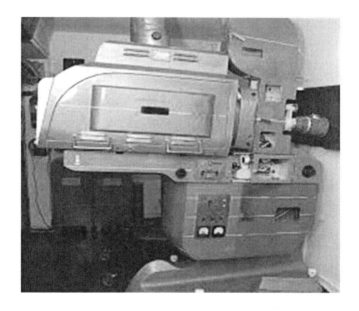

The Embassy

This cinema was sited directly opposite the Broadway. This was another of my favourite haunts as it had a massive auditorium that seemed to go upward forever. There were over 2,500 seats and the Embassy did many 'live' stage shows and always a Christmas pantomime. However, film was my preferred choice, and with their latest magnetic stereophonic sound system, on my days off, you would find me there. Quite often I would be there in the afternoon and then across the road to The Broadway in the evening.

The Odeon

My Uncle John was a projectionist here, so between the Embassy and the Broadway this was my next favourite place depending on who had the film I wanted to see. In that era, different film companies were associated with the two main cinema chains – Rank and ABC.

John would often leave me a free ticket at the box office when he was on duty, and I would spend time in their projection room which always seemed so posh compared with a small suburban one. They all wore white coats which made me so jealous. I used to go back to base and bemoan the fact as I only had an old hand me down khaki one.

The Princess

This was Peterborough's only purpose-built suburban cinema. It opened on 22 July, 1929 with the silent film *Q Ships*. It was a single-floor cinema with a stage and two dressing rooms. The Odeon circuit bought the Princess Cinema in January 1936, but leased it to the J.F. Emery Circuit of Manchester. Odeon then built their own cinema on Broadway in the city centre.

The Princess Cinema ran until 21 March 1958. I remember it very well. I was 11 years old and can remember running all the way there to watch the show, only to be confronted by a big notice on the front doors saying 'CLOSED'.

After this it later became a furniture store, then it became a garage. This saw the front of the building and the projection suite demolished.

In 1992 it became a garden and accessories showroom. However, the latest picture taken in 2012 shows it to have become 'Machine Mart'.

The Princess building as it later became

Those are the cinemas that influenced and guided me to a lifetime in cinema. At the age of 12, I managed to secure a job in a suburban backstreet independent cinema. Just a couple of after school evenings per week, but from that point I started the learning process that was endless.

Chapter Three
New England Cinema

So, I returned to Peterborough to live with my grandparents who lived in the New England district.

The Working Men's Club was built in 1902 and the upper public hall/concert room used as a cinema from February 1913. Originally known as Osborne's Cinema, operated by Mr J. Osborne of Walworth, London. It was called the New England Cinema in 1914. By 1926, Arthur Alderman and his family were in charge. After negotiating the lease from the property owners, Peter Brotherhoods Ltd, they operated the cinema for 40 years.

The projection room was behind the half-moon window at the very top of the building and I used to spend hours looking out across the New England area as the rewind bench was directly behind that window and it was my job to rewind each reel of film back to the beginning ready for its next showing.

Morrison sound was introduced in 1931 and CinemaScope from 10 October 1955.

Mr Arthur Alderman, manager and leaseholder of the New England Cinema, working at one of his CinemaScope projectors. The metal casing houses the carbons, the light from which is concentrated onto a concave mirror which produces the projection beam.

I, personally, have so many fond memories of the New England. This was the first cinema that I was to work in and it was very much a case of 'learn from your mistakes'.

In those days film would arrive in cans with numbered reels. How many reels depended on the length of the film. The idea was to take reel one out of the carrying case, keeping it in an upright position, and then place it on a rewind plate so as to transfer it onto a spool. From here you then checked for any imperfections before putting it on a projector.

On one such occasion, good old me, held the reel of film just like a dinner plate and, whoops, the middle of the reel dropped out onto the floor. *What have I done*; I was thinking to myself watching in shock at the remaining film spiralling to the floor from the reel I was holding. Len, my mentor, rushed over and stopped the film from completely unravelling to the floor and took what was left of it off of me. Then began the long laborious job of getting all this tangled film back into a useable reel again. I certainly learnt a valuable lesson that day.

Looking back on it now, the New England was a 'shoe string' operation with Mr Alderman, the owner / manager, Len, projectionist and Mrs Debeau, a cashier. That being said, what cinema would let a 12-year-old work after school in its premises? I counted myself so lucky and immersed myself into the cinema world. It seemed like a palace to me.

One job that I talked Len into doing, involved the screen curtains. These were manually controlled from the side of the screen so they were opened before the customers came in and closed after the show ended, so as to protect the screen from dust particles and the smoky atmosphere that settled during the night. The 'posh' cinemas could open and close their curtains at the beginning and end of each film which added to the magic of the presentation. "Why can't we do that?" I asked Len one evening after the show. Len explained that their curtains were electrically controlled and could be operated from the projection room, whereas we were not so 'technically advanced'.

I talked Len into letting me go down to the screen just before the film started and when it did, I opened the curtains by pulling on the wire cable. I did the same again as the film finished and closed the curtains. I thought this was terrific as we could now be as good as the others. Looking back on it now, I do think Len and Mr Alderman were pleased with the improvement in our presentation, but it may have just been to appease me.

The New England Cinema closed on 22 May 1966 and although I had then moved on to new pastures, it was a very sad day for me as I wasn't there for Christopher Lee in *Dracula Prince Of darkness,* its final film programme, the closing of the cinema concluded with the retirement of Mr Alderman.

The New England Cinema after its demise in 1966

From 1971–1982, adult films and Asian fare for the local community returned under the name Imperial Cinema. The building then turned full circle, becoming the New England Working Men's Club in 2014.

Chapter Four
The Grand

After the demise of my grandfather, I left Peterborough and returned to the family home in Ramsey. Whilst here, I worked for a short period of time at the Grand.

The Grand Cinema, Ramsey was opened in December 1935. It was built and operated by the Murkett Brothers. The cinema suffered some damage during World War II and the facade was modified. It had a 35-feet wide proscenium. The Grand Cinema was taken over by new operators in 1958, Mr Bill Hadden and his son, Peter.

I worked here between 1964–65 as the one and only projectionist. This was my first experience as a solo projectionist. At 17 I had my first taste of being the one responsible for all things technical in operating a cinema, but during my 18 months working there, I never did feel comfortable or had any sense of achievement. I came to realise that the cinema was just trundling along, as was I.

After much deliberation, I decided to return back to Peterborough and New England as circumstances there had changed, and this being my first initial work experience venue, loyalty guided me to take this backward step.

The Grand had started to struggle with the demise of cinema audiences (that didn't take a lot of working out), but even after leaving, I kept a keen interest on all the different guises The Grand took on to keep the business afloat.

They had some successes in later years. Bingo was tried out, but films soon returned. The rear stalls floor was levelled out to create a bar area. The front stalls seating was removed and the area used by the community as a disco at certain times, with the audience for films being seated in the balcony only.

During its later stages the Grand made several attempts to encourage people to use the cinema's facilities, some more bizarre than others. Indoor market stalls for a 'bring and buy sale'. A screening of the film *Grease* for a private party that wanted to dance to the film whilst it was showing. However, and this one beggar belief, the press headlines read like this:

'Nude audiences are helping to keep a cinema in business! A Sunday screening of the film *Calendar Girls* has been arranged with a naturists club.'

The adverts for this event carried the message 'as cinema seats can be rough, bring something soft to sit on!' you just gotta laugh.

I look back now and find it astounding that years later, my son, Stuart, followed my footsteps into the cinema business and found himself working for Peter Haddon, primarily at the Cromwell Cinema in Huntingdon, but also did a few stand-in shifts at The Grand.

Although his love of cinema most likely comes from me, his love for music and song writing is a mystery, but I still vividly remember how proud Gerry and I were attending, as part of a packed house, a live Christmas show of 'Stuart in Concert' at The Grand.

The Grand Cinema closed on 17 June 2005 after it was purchased by the local council to be re-developed, with proposed housing to be built on the site.

Now just a distant memory, and another cinema bites the dust. This is now the site where the Grand once stood and a new generation will never know of its existence. It is now the town's public library and a residential area.

Chapter Five
Abbeygate 1966–1970

Leaving home at 19 years of age to start a new life in Bury St Edmunds was to be a huge milestone in my life. This wasn't like moving to Peterborough, which was just a small bus ride away. I was just a young, naïve teenager leaving family and friends behind to move forward to an unknown destination. Daunting though it felt at the time, looking back now I believe it was most likely my destiny within life's rich pattern.

From my very first day at the Abbeygate Cinema, I felt at ease and had this uncanny feeling of belonging. It's difficult to explain really as I threw myself headlong into this new venture from the moment I had settled in to my new surroundings and lifestyle.

I needed to know more about The Abbeygate and its former history and started questioning anyone that had knowledge of the years before I came on the scene and could relate the history to me.

Mr Hugh Berry was the general manager of that time, and someone I took an instant liking to when I met him some two weeks earlier. I had been invited to attend an interview to cover the vacant projectionist post and I believe he saw the potential within me.

Hugh was a confirmed bachelor and lived in a small flat within the cinema property. Often when he was on a day off, he would invite me to spend my midshift break with him. I think this was just so he had some company as he lived on his own, but I also enjoyed having someone I could talk to who shared the same interest in cinema as I did. It was during these times we would discuss the cinema's history, but, funnily enough, not its future projections. Strangely enough in the mid-1960s, life and work seemed a little static and it wasn't until a few years later those changes started to come by thick and fast.

Hugh had a very similar introduction into cinema life as I did and when we related our own experiences starting out, it was almost uncanny how we both had followed the same footpath. His story, though, started many years earlier than mine.

He had worked his way into the projection room of the long-forgotten Gainsborough Cinema in Sudbury, Suffolk, back in 1932. He was still there when he became conscripted for National Service. During this daunting time, his cinema interest and experience as a projectionist got him a posting to the overseas entertainment section. This involved travelling around and providing film shows to troops stationed at different barracks. The back of a lorry became his projection room. In 1952 he became the manager of the Central Cinema in Bury St Edmunds.

This cinema was built in the late 1920s. Earnie Bostock and his son Douglas ran the Bostock circuit which was based in Ipswich, Suffolk. They looked toward Bury St Edmunds to expand their business and decided to buy up this select residential property in Hatter Street. Looking at the above picture now, for the life of me, I still can't get my head around how a person could walk up this side street, well off the town centre and think to themselves, *I'll build a cinema here!* although I'm very glad that they did.

Thereafter, the long arduous task of turning this property into an entertainment centre began. After many setbacks and delays in converting and designing the ground floor, the cinema entrance succeeded to hide the fact that a 600-seat auditorium lay within.

In its early years, the Central was a mix of Music Hall live shows with film interludes projected from a rear-screen projection room. The rear of this building was badly damaged by fire in 1930. After this, live acts were cancelled. A new projection room was built above the rear of the entrance foyer and the Central became a full-time cinema. This then set the scene for the next 25 years. Although, in its latter years it became known locally as 'The Flea Pit'.

In 1955, a Kent businessman, Harold B. Millar, bought up the lease of The Central along with the Exchange cinema in Dereham, Norfolk, which had the same landlord. This business venture was entitled 'Kinemas East Anglia Group'.

The Central was to have a complete and well overdue re-modernisation and a name change to Abbeygate Cinema. This name was to give it some credence to being situated within the historic core of the town and a turning off Abbeygate Street, the main through road that leads down to the Abbey gateway and Abbey Gardens. This also segregated it from its past history.

To herald the event, a gala opening was held in December 1959 with the cast of the new satire comedy *Please Turn Over* headed by Ted Ray and Leslie Phillips in attendance. The Abbeygate thrived very nicely and became a respected name within the cinema fraternity.

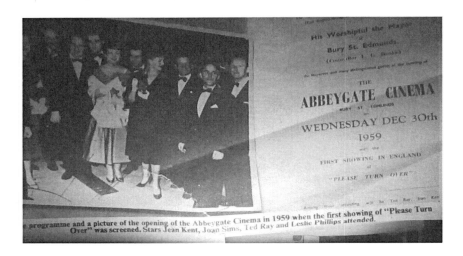

programme and a picture of the opening of the Abbeygate Cinema in 1959 when the first showing of "Please Turn Over" was screened. Stars Jean Kent, Joan Sims, Ted Ray and Leslie Phillips attended.

So, with all of that history behind it, in February 1966, I came on the scene as the assistant projectionist and, from the very start, my learning cycle started off all over again.

Cinema operation at that time was a fairly routine setup and the same running order for nearly every cinema regardless of location. The week would start on Sunday with a mediocre title, showing for one day, usually a re-run of some re-issued older film. Monday, for three days, would see the less popular titles (and there were many of these) or films that had played earlier and gained attention via word of mouth etc. Thursday, Friday and Saturday would be reserved for the pick of the week title.

When the more quality film came out, it would run for seven days and if we were really lucky, for two weeks, but rarely any longer. If it was really good, it would make a comeback as a re-issue about a year later, once the City Centre sites had finished with it. During that period there were no other outlets for film presentation, so re-issues were a common occurrence.

This practice remained unchanged for several years and became the projectionist staple diet, mostly consisting of film handling work. There was always plenty of that to do especially on the Monday of each week.

Monday was film delivery/collection day. On odd occasions when a film was missing, panic phone calls would be made to the film distributors in London and copies of the film would be hastily sent out on trains to the town that required them. I lost count, the many times I had to fetch two, or even three cases of film from the parcels office of our local railway station and then had to trudge back to the cinema with them perched on my trusty sack barrow.

Although, operationally everything was fairly routine, my personal life hit a major change and I started courting a local girl who lived in one of the flats which were adjacent to the Abbeygate. My lonely life certainly gave way to another purpose and I never looked back.

Back in Ramsey, it came as a complete shock to my parents that a girlfriend was on the scene. I have said before, they always thought of me as a backroom film junkie living this imaginary celluloid life from the confines of a dark old projection room, but once this girl came into my life (the real thing), I didn't hang about.

Within a year we were married and I realised that my new-found responsibilities would have an impact on my life. My working life in the cinema would have to adjust, but only slightly. This was not all that difficult, as just being the assistant projectionist meant I could arrange time off to suit my different domestic chores.

However, this setup didn't last very long as the chief projectionist left the following year and I was promoted to that position. Obviously, the workload intensified with the extra responsibilities and there always seemed to be a staff shortage.

Cinema projection work was not seen as the ideal career move during that time and had the knock-on effect that projectionists of any quality were few and far between. The 'good old chief' was expected to cover all eventualities which in turn meant one's domestic life was sometimes hard to juggle. Luckily, I had chosen the right girl to share the burden with me and we could always find something to laugh about, whatever the situation (some 54 years later we still laugh). She even came on board and did some evening usherette work, mainly to help out with the family budget. I can still vividly remember seeing her walk down the auditorium during the interval with an ice cream tray whilst I lit her up with a spotlight. She actually loved doing that and do you know, even now, she still loves doing it during all our 'live show' presentations that have half-time intermissions. Just about every person there calls her by her name 'Two strawberry ones, please Gerry'.

After only 18 months of being the 'Chief Projectionist', it was suddenly announced that the Abbeygate was being sold to The Star Group of Companies for a complete re-modelling and a new future, but our jobs would continue as part of the deal. This saw owner Mr Miller bow out, leaving us all wondering just what lay ahead.

Chapter Six

Studios 1&2 // Bingo Social Club
1970–1985

Later that day when I was home explaining the recent events to the missus, I suddenly remembered that sometime back whilst I had been looking up the history of the Savoy Cinema, Newark-on-Trent, the name Star Group had come to light. They had also been the owners of this cinema. Knowing this, I was spurred into wanting some insight as to who this company was and how they had come into being.

It transpired that this company was headed by the Eckart brothers, Derek and Rodney (and I don't mean the 'Trotters', although it could well have been). Their offices were based at Cavendish House in Leeds and it soon became obvious that this company would have no respect for the historic core of the Abbeygate. As I looked over their portfolio of all the sites they owned, one thing stood out alarmingly – the majority of their cinema stock consisted of old single-screen sites that were being sold off cheaply for one reason or another, but mostly due to the steady decline in regular cinemagoers. As a company, their aim was to split the building into small multiple units depending on building size, rename them all uniformly (Studios 1 – 2 – etc) and then take the larger majority of the building and turn it into the latest money-making craze of the era, a bingo hall.

The Abbeygate closed its doors for one of these conversions, and although the manager and two projectionists were kept on to oversee and learn the new equipment that would be forthcoming, the rest of the staff were laid off with the promise of re-employment upon completion. This was a bitter blow for myself and Gerry, as the extra income from her job as usherette had stabilised the family budget.

It was sad, and yet, dare I say it, exciting to see the old building carved up and rebuilt into a different guise.

The projectionist role was about to dramatically change. The days of having two projectors showing single reels of film and changing over to individual parts throughout the performance were gone. Our only two 'new' pieces of equipment were the 'Tower' innovation systems. These larger than life spools would hold a full programme. No more standing by a projector, waiting to do a changeover. These 'large reels' could carry a full feature. Once the show was up and running, they didn't really need any attention until the end of the show. However, this relied heavily upon all the different pieces of equipment behaving themselves. All our original equipment was adapted and re-used, but over the next few years we went through several different projectors as they just couldn't stand up to the continuous running that was now required of them. We always seemed to end up with some other cinema's cast-offs.

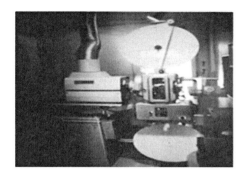

The different projectors that got worn out here was unbelievable

Our biggest headache was the projectionist curse of the 'Periscope' system. This required the image upon leaving the projector to be beamed onto an angled mirror. The image was then reflected down onto an even larger mirror which then reflected the image on to the screen. As I am sure you can imagine, the complexity of sending the image from the projector through a series of mirrors to the screen meant that the mirrors required cleaning and adjusting on a regular basis. Failure to maintain this would lead to a noticeable decline in picture quality.

This system also meant that you couldn't see the audience below anymore; in fact, you could not even see a full-screen unless you were pressed up against the porthole.

The newly converted 'Studios 1 and 2' used a 'Periscope system' in both of their screens, hence the reason in becoming a nightmare. After several years of maintaining the periscope system in 'Studio 1', we finally managed to coerce the company into building a separate projection room. This was mounted to the side of the building and supported on concrete stilts. This then made way for the removal of those 'blasted mirrors' and the dismantling of the periscope shaft.

The picture quality improved so much with the introduction of 'direct' projection.

The construction of 'Studio 1'
Projection Room

There are very few periscope systems in operation today, but our setup in Screen 2 is still going strong after many years of tender loving care.

Over the years, whilst the construction of the building has never allowed us to pursue other alternatives, technology has changed dramatically. The digital projection era has introduced much smaller and quieter projection equipment.

Direct projection is no longer a pipe dream for our Screen 2 as we are looking at siting a new projector in the void where the 'periscope' mirrors are currently housed (There is a God up there, he's just been a little slow getting to me).

Meanwhile, back to my story and the challenge of two screens in the same building. Not only had the machinery for showing films changed, another new addition to our equipment involved the light source used to project the image to the screen.

Up until 1970, I had been using carbon arc light. This was produced by two copper rods, a negative and a positive, burning against each other to produce a bright light. However, these couldn't run a great length of time without being adjusted and since we could now run a complete feature without changing projector, a new system was required.

The xenon lamp is a highly specialised type of gas discharge lamp. Still used today, it is an electric light that is more even and brighter than a carbon one and, as long as it is kept cool, will last 1000 hours and beyond. It still operates under the same principle as a carbon in that the light is directly in front of a concave mirror which beams it onto the picture frame.

Exciting though that it was to have this whole new operation in place, believe it or not, there was a downside.

The amount of film work had decreased, despite there being two screens to look after. With the new 'Tower' systems in place, once up and running, it was a case of machine-minding until the reel ran out which would be the end of the performance.

The projection room had become a very isolated and lonely place to be in. Whereas in previous days with the old two projector system, there would often be two projectionists in attendance, this new system only required one projectionist. Although I didn't know it then, looking back, this was the beginning of the decline of a proper projectionist who looked after the film presentation.

Today, in this digital age, all that is required is a fully computerised, unmanned projection room. The performance is controlled from computers located in other areas of the building. Maintenance is provided via 'updates' sent externally through servers and networks.

Our new look building re-opened on December 16 1971 as Studios 1 & 2 and Social Bingo Club. Looking back on it now, it was probably our saviour. The town still had the 1300-seat Odeon taking half the film releases, but, unlike our newly refurbished building, it was struggling from lack of investment since its opening some 35 years earlier.

Studios 1 & 2 in Hatter Street was now 'The place to watch movies' in Bury St Edmunds.

After the initial opening period with all the 'Razza-ma-taz', the cinema business soon settled into the same level as the rest of the industry at that time, and it soon became quite apparent that bingo was the driving force behind the company. The cinema suffered from there being no management structure. The bingo manager (much to their dislike of anything cinema related) had no choice but to oversee the cinema side of the business. This was a chore that had an 'if and when' mentality about it. This practice went on for the next four years, a dark age in the history of the Hatter Street Cinema. Not only was the business at its lowest ebb, but there was no interest within.

During this time, I was trying hard to keep a stable family life together whilst also trying to be a calming influence on the many cinema issues that were arising. However, this was not so easy when tied up in a projection room at the very top of the building.

At home, my circumstances had changed. I was a now a father and I was finding it even more difficult to maintain a balance between work and home.

Our son, Stuart, was growing up fast and I seemed to spend the next few years settled into a pattern of grabbing a few hours off whenever possible, then getting back before the start of the evening performance. There were the occasional days off every week or so which gave me some family time at home.

Then in January 1985, the owners, Star Group, after some unscrupulous accounting, lost their gaming license and sold off the bingo assets to the EMI chain who were actively looking at this area of the business for themselves. However, taking us on meant we would be a new branch within their organisation, and because they already had the surviving ABC cinemas under their EMI banner, they had no interest in our two small cinema screens. The now depleted Star Group were still going to operate some of their cinema stock that didn't include bingo, but unfortunately our attendances had started to decline and it was decided that the loss-making site at Bury St Edmunds should be boarded up until another use could be found. Logistically, being way out from their Leeds base, it just didn't hold any interest.

Of course, at that time I was only the chief projectionist, but I had been performing many managerial duties behind the scenes over the past few years, so I approached the company and implored them to reconsider. I offered my services to manage the cinema and provided some detailed plans I wanted to implement, but they had made their decision and rejected my offer.

Knowing in my heart that I could, if given the chance, make a success of this site, a campaign was launched to reverse their train of thought, and after several heated meetings they finally gave the go-ahead for us to move forward, and in their own words told me to 'put the money where your mouth is!'

I was given six months to turn the business around on the understanding that, if no sustained improvement was made, it would be 'curtains closed', no questions asked.

So, in February 1975, I took the reins as the general manager of Studios 1&2.

It was a very difficult period as there just wasn't any quality films about to attract that much interest in cinema, but failure was not an option. I had to ensure that we would be pulling out all the stops to promote ourselves to the townsfolk.

We still had neighbourly connections with the bingo hall and its staff. Although the building was now separated and dual access points sealed up, we still shared several areas and facilities. You must remember that it was originally designed as a combined unit. The bingo operation was now managed by Claudine and Albert, a husband and wife team. Before the bingo/cinema split, I had built up a good working relationship with both of them and I was determined to maintain that relationship, regardless of all the company changes. I have fond memories of attending some award presentations for them.

Whilst it was so important to make the cinema successful, my greatest difficulty was trying to maintain a healthy and happy life at home. The demands on my time at the cinema were ever increasing, but my ever-loving family never did put any undue pressure on me. In fact, they supported and encouraged me in everything I did and in return I took every opportunity to share some family time, even if only for short walks or days out, depending on my free time and our son was growing up so fast.

Back at work, I was still overseeing a busy projection room that was sited three floors up at the very top of the building. Luckily enough, we did have a good communication system between floor levels, but some days it was a struggle running up and down which often seemed to correspond with both areas needing you at the same time.

On the home front we had managed to juggle our domestic problems into letting my mother-in-law look after our son Stuart who was now two years old and becoming quite a character of his own. Two years old? Where had that time gone?

For years, my mother-in-law had been quite a recluse, except for her visits to us. Looking after Stuart seemed to give her a whole new purpose in life. Being a widow, living a solitary existence, she suddenly had a new outlook on life. The situation was ideal and allowed Gerry to come back and do some part time cashier work at the cinema. It proved to be a good move as she began to understand some of the problems I was having, trying to hold everything together.

With my wife on board, along with the rest of my team, our first major change was put into place. We wanted to make the now shabby-looking entrance more inviting and attractive. With the help of my trusty toolbox, we all got mucked in and spruced up our foyer and kiosk area. After a couple of weeks, everyone involved was so pleased with the result that the feeling of enthusiasm set in. "What's next?" they kept asking.

One of the better things we achieved was the introduction of Westlers Hot Dogs. If you can remember them, they were so popular, it was a job of its own just to keep up with the sales, especially if we got taken by surprise with a lot more customers than expected. The bread rolls where delivered in bulk once a week. Each of us would take turns to slice them across the top so as to take the frankfurter, then re-pack and place in the freezer until needed. On any unexpected busy periods, we would have bread rolls thawing out everywhere you could possibly imagine. The top of the radiators was the most favourite spot. On one particular evening, a customer came out of the cinema and looked as if he was about to complain (oh oh what have we done), when he announced that he had expected the roll and frankfurter to be hard like it had been in other cinemas. He had bitten down on it so hard and had jarred his teeth.

"I want another one," was his main statement. Wow.

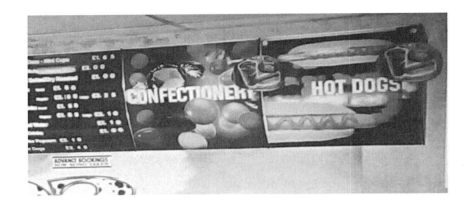

Whilst on the subject of cinema snacks, popcorn has always been a mystery to me; the second most popular selling product in cinemas across the globe (after soft drinks), to me, it was always a blessing and a curse.

The profit margin from this product was huge, but the clean up after busy performances became an absolute nightmare. How on Earth this became a staple diet for cinemagoers, I will never know. Personally, I hate the stuff and I'm sure I'm not alone with that view. I can't stand the taste of it, the smell of it or even the look of it. If I have a nightmare, it invariably involves sold out performances and popcorn everywhere. When I say 'everywhere', I mean everywhere. After a busy performance we would find it wedged down the side of seat cushions, under the seats in the most inaccessible of places and, of course, tonnes of it trodden into the carpet between the rows of seats.

We used to sell it in 3 different varieties – sweet, salted and toffee. Sweet and salted was always served 'warm', whilst the toffee popcorn was pre-bagged. Sweet popcorn, once warm after being held in someone's hand for a period of time, would become sticky and would cling to everything. Toffee popcorn and sweet popcorn, once trodden into carpet, was an absolute nightmare to hoover up. It would form a sticky ball and the hoover pipe would always become blocked.

The salt popcorn was so light and fluffy that it seemed to have a mind of its own. It would float and spread so much further. I hate the bloody stuff, always have done and always will! On a plus though, at least we didn't serve the hot butter to pour on top of it. Could you imagine the mess that would have caused?

The worst scenario would be after a kids' matinee, with a very limited time to clean up before the next show was due in. I'm sure the kids only ever bought it so they could have 'popcorn fights' with their friends. These performances got so bad that instead of using hoovers, I invested in heavy duty Garden Leaf collection machines. These had much more of an effect in a quick clean up time and very rarely clogged up.

Anyway, back to the story of Star.

The company and all its cinemas supported wholeheartedly the industry charity the 'Variety Club of Great Britain' and we were no exception in collecting and holding different events for the cause.

It was very heart-warming to receive a certificate which I could relay to all the staff and patrons alike.

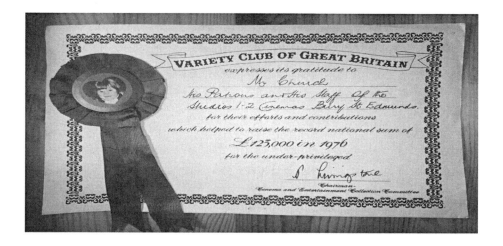

Studios 1-2 Bury St Edmunds was at last being recognised on its own merits. Spurred on by this success, we had a film coming up that was a cut well above the mediocre fare that we had been subject to over the past months, it was:

'A Passage to India'

Based on E.M. Forster's novel of the same name, the film was directed by David Lean and starred, among many others, Nigel Havers.

Nigel Havers, we found out was in Suffolk at the time, so we hastily wrote to the film distributors asking if he would be available and willing to promote the film here at our cinema. With the help of the film company, they passed our request onto his agent, and lo and behold, the date was set. What a scoop it made. The opening night was so special; plus, the publicity it created gave us a very successful run.

It was during this time I found myself in constant pain and discomfort, but managed it foolishly, so it seemed to keep it from everyone else around me, until I got rumbled, so to speak. Gerry had me straight up the doctor's and the outcome was a gallbladder problem. After being sent to see the specialist, his diagnosis was that it had to be removed without delay.

Ten days later, there I was in hospital for the operation. When I voiced my complaints to Gerry that I would be away from my cinema for a week, you should have heard the comments, though, perhaps not. They were not very complementary!

Whist recovering, I came into contact with someone that would become my closest friend, John Arnold.

We came together quite by chance really as his wife Sandra came to join our team at the cinema and we would meet and exchange pleasantries on occasions when he would come to meet her from work.

Over the next year we became close friends and our relationship felt much akin to two brothers. We were both interested in and followed snooker and so we made Tuesday mornings, whenever possible, our 'snooker mornings' by joining up with the Pot Black Snooker Club for a couple of hours playtime, and what fun we had. It turned out to be just what I needed to recharge the batteries, so to speak, from the rigours of day to day problems.

We even had our very own mini table top version for when it wasn't possible to get out to play.

Unfortunately, John was a victim of muscular atrophy and some days really suffered, but it never dulled his sense of humour. We had so much fun and laughter with him and his wife, Sandra, and their two lovely daughters, Tracy and Vicki. We even managed to go on holiday together as an extended family.

As time wore on, John became confined to a wheelchair, but even that couldn't daunt him, and we managed to get away on a day trip to London so he could fulfil his wish to go on the London Eye.

John was taken away from us at the very early age of 57, a bitter blow that was hard to bear. I've never picked up a snooker cue since.

Chapter Seven

Although I never had the privilege of working in this building, it would be wrong not to mention the Odeon Cinema, which, for many years, was classed as 'the opposition'.

This purpose-built cinema played a large part in keeping the cinematic interest alive to the populate of Suffolk. I was a regular visitor to this cinema, either to sit and watch a show, or spend time in the projection room. Little did I know then, but, in that projection room, I met someone that would become such an important factor in the future success of the Hatter Street Cinema. However, more importantly, he would become a very close friend of mine.

Frank Edgeley

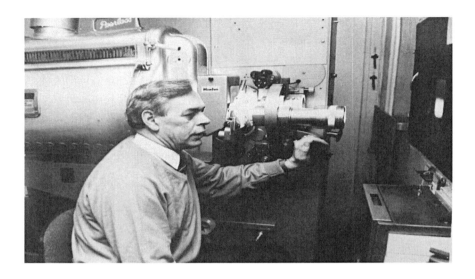

Frank had spent his life in cinema and always had some fascinating stories to tell. In his earlier days, he could always be seen riding around town on his Triumph motorbike and often visited the Abbeygate projection room.

It was during my first weeks at the Abbeygate that I met up with Frank and we soon became colleagues and friends. He would talk of the other long-gone cinema of the town, The Playhouse, and would divulge into all of the amateur dramatic antics they got up to.

After leaving school at the tender age of just 14, he secured a position working in Whipps Fresh Fish shop in Abbeygate Street. Here he developed a passion for dressing crabs. He would tell me, with great relish, that every time he had a fresh crab to dress and gave me all the gory details of the process, probably because he knew I didn't like them.

He started off his cinema career by becoming a rewind boy at the Central Cinema, and all the menial tasks that went with the job, like having to fill the managers coal scuttle up each day. He eventually climbed the rocky path to chief projectionist at the Playhouse Cinema until its demise.

Frank then moved on to the Odeon and took great pride in being the head projectionist there. I would often pay a visit and watch his show in that immaculate projection room that he took great pride in. He remained there until the building was sold to the Brent Walker group and was re-named 'Focus'. Not long after this take over though, Frank could see the writing on the wall and a change of venue was required. Luckily, fate was about to show its hand once again.

As previously mentioned, Frank had begun his cinema life as a rewind boy at The Central, so he jumped at the chance to return to his roots and join us for his remaining working years at the building that had started his career off. I often wonder if he realised at that time just what challenge he had let himself in for.

At the time of his return, we were going through a very difficult transition period and fighting for our very own survival to become recognised and accepted by a brand new company.

Frank came on board and brought with him his many years of expertise. This experience was tested to the ultimate maximum as we mobilised to undertake an in-house modernisation programme. The idea was to renovate the cinema ourselves, using materials from cinemas that were already being closed in the hope of overturning a pending closure ourselves.

We drove miles, collecting seats, carpets and projection spares. We worked side by side to transform the cinema (spending as little money as possible) and devoted all of our time to show the 'execs' of the company how important this small-screen operation was to us and the town of Bury St Edmunds. Frank's enthusiasm and input was a big factor in saving this cinema.

Accolades followed and I was so pleased and deeply proud to see all of Frank's hard work and enthusiasm recognised by all the hierarchy of the company. It reflected all of the hard work myself and the entire team had achieved in keeping this small, two-screen cinema, in Bury St Edmunds operating and overturning a period of cinema attendance decline.

Frank always met any new form of technology with enthusiasm and relish, but he got quite despondent at the lack of presentation in the later years.

Presentation was everything to Frank and woe betide anyone that upset his well-rehearsed pattern of putting a picture on the screen in the correct way. As the man behind the scenes he would often say, "If I'm not thought of, then everything must be going well."

Credits roll for Frank

AFTER a cinema career spanning 50 years in Bury St Edmunds man is retiring.

Frank Edgeley, 65, of Samuel Street Walk, has been the chief technician at the Odeon cinema in Bury for 35 years but started his career at the Central in 1953.

Mr Edgeley said he would miss his job. "I don't really want to retire, I love this job, it feels sad to be leaving after all these years," he said.

"If I could go back in time I would not change anything I have loved every minute of my work."

Even after viewing thousands of films at work, he still enjoys watching a video at home with his wife Jo, who he met at the Playhouse in 1957 where she worked as a usherette.

Manager of the Odeon Pat Church said: "I have had a very good working relationship with Frank.

"Frank will be a really hard act to follow with all the knowledge that he has amassed over the years."

END OF AN ERA: Frank Edgeley is retiring from the Odeon cinema in Bury St Edmunds after 50 years in the business   0301-202-40   Picture by Angela Sharpe

By the time Frank finally retired, he had become an Odeon employee once again. Far from the days of the old Odeon / Focus building, new digital and satellite projection methods started to see the true projectionist position fade away.

When Frank died in 2009, it was truly the end of an amazing era. We had joined forces and kept the cinema going from strength to strength.

"From everyone who has enjoyed a good film from your projector Frank, God Bless!"

Chapter Eight

The team was now complete and paved the way for some busy times ahead. Suddenly it seemed there was some better product coming from the studios and film had got a kick start.

When the North Wind Blows started the ball rolling; it was our biggest blockbuster for many years, mainly due to the advent of TV advertising. Audiences started to flock to the cinema, and being 'Sold Out' was about to become normal practice. We hit a sustainable run, one good film after another. *Across the Great Divide*, *Grease* and not forgetting the one and only *Jaws*.

Whilst all this had been going on, home life had been very intermittent. Our son was still growing up fast and had expressed a talent for playing and writing music. This was something that completely mesmerised and astonished me every time I heard him. I always took time out from my busy schedule to take him to piano lessons each week.

Gerry and I were such proud parents when he was accepted into the Cathedral Choir, however this always caused me a little internal turmoil, as I could not get to many of the concert events he was involved with. They always seemed to coincide with my workload, but we always made up for it when we were together as a family. We would arrange little house parties and watch him perform his own music. He was in his element and so were we.

Back at the cinema, we had just gone through the past six months of exceptionally busy films and it had taken its toll on the building. The screens had taken such a battering and now looked so tired and worn out. The company's attitude was just 'Take, Take, Take!' Nothing was being put back into our business operation and all requests for any improvements fell on deaf ears.

We decided that this could no longer continue and began to put our own plans into operation to see if we could, at a site level, improve on everything that we had to offer. If the company wouldn't roll out a refurbishment for us, we would have to do it ourselves.

As luck would have it, around this time, the Odeon/Focus closed its doors, ready for demolition, to make way for a shopping complex.

Frank still had contacts within that building and we were given permission to remove anything that was left over after the strip-out, to re-use and improve our operation.

During the next few weeks, we could often be seen struggling down the street with all odd pieces of technical equipment, furnishings and fittings which we would store away for future use.

It was such a sad day to see this happen to a building that had stood there, so majestic, for all those years.

Looking at these pictures now brought back memories from the day when Frank and myself got in and took down all the ceiling light fittings from under the circle. We then spent many loving hours drilling holes in the sides of them and putting coloured Cinemoid over to make them look more decorative once in their new position. We were somewhat chuffed with the outcome, though it probably meant nothing to anyone else. It was our small dedication to another passing cinema.

30 years later, what really pleases me is that after several different ownerships and alterations, I have always managed to keep those lights. The next time anyone is in the Abbeygate Screen 1 or 2, look to the ceiling and you will see a little bit of cinema history.

As I said earlier, with the increase in audiences, more performances a day were required. This had a devastating effect on our projection equipment. We had worn out so many projectors and it was a constant battle to try to maintain them. We were always trying to get the company to invest in something more updated, but it always seemed to fall on deaf ears and that didn't do anything to ease our frustrations.

Although it was always an uphill battle, I never did get despondent with the current situation. Had I let myself get frustrated with the operation and the current company running it, it would have had a detrimental effect on the rest of the team.

We were working with utensils and equipment that was thoroughly worn out by the day to day operation and our customers were starting to notice.

We had just started to run the film, *Gremlins*. This had seen so much publicity at the time as it had been certified too 'nasty' for children to see, even though, predominately, it was aimed at that very age group. Everyone was talking about it. This led to large audiences flocking to see just what all the fuss was about. It also meant that we had to expand our running times to accommodate the increase in business.

Our projectors were the first to rebel against the added pressure and kept malfunctioning at inopportune moments.

In those days, the local newspaper used to send a regular correspondent each week to get the programme information for the week ahead (remember, this was way before the days of Ceefax, Oracle and Online information!). I happened to let slip that our equipment was struggling, almost as if it had developed its own Gremlins, causing havoc with our presentations.

That week, the 'Bury Free Press' hit the streets with a story entitled 'Gremlins in the Works'. This was cleverly phrased to give an insight to hide our plight of worn out equipment. Suddenly, our customers started to feel sorry for us. 'It wasn't the cinema's fault, it was those rotten Gremlins.'

Two days after this story was published in the press, my office phone burst into life. The conversation that followed is still so surreal to me, but as I lifted the receiver to my ear, I heard the most American voice I could have ever imagined say, "Is that Mr Pat Church, the guy who's fighting off Gremlins infesting his cinema? This is Radio L.A. and we are 'LIVE'. Tell me and all of my listeners, what the heck is going on over there?"

Stunned, though I was, I spoke about five minutes of made-up improvisation (I was not going to impart that the equipment was at fault as it was so worn out). The interviewer ended with a hearty laugh and I was left on the end of the phone, completely bewildered. How the hell had a radio station in L.A. got to know about this?

With everything run down and depleted, frustration had really set in. The company wouldn't invest, and we were desperately trying to keep the cinema presentable by using other, deceased cinemas' cast offs.

Then, suddenly and unexpectedly, we received news that the Star Group had sold out to Cannon Cinemas.

Chapter Nine
Cannon 1985–1992

There was a new name on the cinema exhibition circuit in the UK. I had been following this company from the trade magazines over the past couple of years. It was headed by two Israeli cousins, Menahem Golan and Yoram Globus. They started out by basing themselves in Los Angeles and started making many exploitation movies along with a few better-quality films just to give them some credence. This earned them the industry nick name, 'The Go Go Boys'.

Their aim was to flood the market with their own branded product, then to branch into the UK; they bought up two struggling cinema chains, the Classic Cinemas from Lew Grade and the Studio Cinemas from the Eckarts. Their intention was to rename these cinemas after a modernisation programme, 'Cannon Cinemas'. This provided them with an outlet that wouldn't be subject to other film companies prejudices.

My very first encounter with anyone from this company didn't fair too well as their first overall opinion of our cinema was that it was way too small for them to be interested in, and its general condition would not make it worthy of the investment required to bring it up to the expected Cannon standards. For the foreseeable future we were to continue to operate under the Studios 1&2 banner until the final decision was made. However, we were to expect and prepare to be closed down and boarded up until another use could be found.

I had the task of relaying this message back to all the staff that had been waiting to hear what the future had in store for us all. We all had expected some capital investment into our cinema so you can imagine just what a difficult meeting it was – relaying all those negative comments back.

Once the initial shock was over, we all agreed that we should not let all the hard work we had done in collecting the parts and materials from the old Odeon go to waste. We decided to make an effort to go ahead with our original plans to spruce up the place with our very own DIY attributes. If Cannon wouldn't consider us a viable operation, perhaps another exhibitor would. We were not prepared to let them put us down without a fight.

And so, work began in earnest on improving our site. On the plus side, I knew many of the Star personal that were still with Cannon, and of the cinemas that had already gone into the refurbishment stage. I put out feelers that if the seats, carpets, drapes etc. were in a re-useable condition, we would like to have them. The favourable replies that came back meant that Frank and I travelled all over in a hire van, collecting whatever we could lay our hands on. This made all the in-house work more worthwhile.

The hierarchy of the company looked on in amazement at all this activity as it was completely out of the ordinary for a team to take it upon themselves to refurbish their own site. This was above and beyond the normal day to day operation of a cinema.

After three months of working every hour we could, the job was nearing completion and our future was still very undecided. Every time I made enquiries, it was always met with the words, "Let's just wait and see, be patient."

BEFORE   *AFTER*

On completion of our refurbishment, we were all feeling so pleased with ourselves, and why not. The accolades from our patrons made all the hard work so worthwhile. More or less upon the completion of our 'Do It Yourself' refurb, I was informed that the Cannon yearly conference was in six weeks' time and I would be expected to join them and, 'Oh yes, this year it's being held in Majorca.' What a shock this was; as it would be my very first time abroad, and as details of travel arrangements started to filter through, excitement and tension started to mount.

The day of departure saw me, full of apprehension, make the drive from Bury St Edmunds to Birmingham Airport, then it was 'Up, Up and Away'. It was a strange experience and everything was so different to anything else I had experienced. Then, during a management meeting session, it was announced that our cinema in Bury St Edmunds would be joining the Cannon family and all new livery would be put in place upon my return. During dinner that very same evening, I was presented with a Cannon logo tie, much to my roommate's delight.

The week passed by at breakneck speed. I attended several workshop talks and meetings which were usually followed by tours to local beauty spots and free time to do one's own thing, it was a mini holiday really. The conference culminated with the Gala Dinner. This was the highlight of the week as all the accolades and awards were presented. During the award ceremony, the managing director, Barry Jenkins, gave a short speech regarding the 'David Pratt' trust for the benefit of all the newcomers as he put it. David had been the previous managing director, but had died suddenly in office in 1983 at a tragically early age. As a permanent memorial for his love of children, a trust was set up for the upkeep and purchase of 'Sunshine Coaches' in his name, as part of the Variety Club of Great Britain. The 'David Pratt' award always recognised cinemas that had gone above and beyond the call of duty. His next sentence took my breath away, "Would Mr Pat Church from Bury St Edmunds come to the stage and accept this year's honour." As I walked across the room, on very shaky legs, my only thought was of everyone back at home. This was their honour for all the work and effort they had done to get us to this point.

DAVID PRATT AWARD

This year's David Pratt Award, giving to the person who, in the opinion of the Directors, has done outstanding work for the Trust, went to Pat Church of Bury St Edmunds, and on the right we see him receiving it from Barry Jenkins.

VARIETY CLUB AWARDS

I returned home and relished breaking the good news that we would become a Cannon cinema and that there was no more threat of closure. All the hard work everyone had put in had paid off. Shortly after this, we had all the signage replaced and began to promote our new identity to the people.

Over the next year we did everything we could think of to promote our new name to our public. I think the highlight of our endeavours was me dressing up as Fievel, a character from a new film that was about to open, and joining the Bury carnival crowds during the town's festive season. It was something so different from what we would normally do, but seeing the happy faces of all those children made it all worthwhile. We also had several kids' competitions and charity fundraising events that gained us some favourable press coverage and put the name 'Cannon cinemas' well into the forefront for all to recognise.

This picture just goes to show what exciting things can happen when you win a Scoop Squad competition.

These lucky members won tickets to see films at Cannon Cinemas One and Two in Bury St Edmunds.

Not only were they presented with their tickets when they went to the cinema, but they chatted to Mr Pat Church the manager, were shown round the project room and were given special books from the film-makers.

Chief projectionist Mr Frank Edgley is pictured in the back row with Mr Church on his right.

The back row of Scoop members, from left, are: Christopher Snelling, Sarah Jane Green, Edward Nobbs, Stuart Pearce and John Chenery.

Suzanne Plummer and Luke Allard are in the front row.

Well done

Successful stamp collectors, Kelly and Lindsay Moss and Sharon and Clare Pearce, share the prize for being the biggest Scoop Squad contributors to our stamp appeal.

Between them Kelly and Lindsay, of 9 Avenue Approach, Bury St Edmunds and Sharon and Clare, of The Greyhound, Ixworth, collected well over 10,000 stamps, with Sharon and Clare totting up 6,386!

The girls won a free seat at the Studios Cinema in Bury to see the great new film The Never Ending Story.

A big thank you to all our other members who gave stamps to the appeal — I have sent them off for sale in enormous bags, so

I should soon know how much money we have raised. Thank you too to all the members of the public who kept the stamps flowing in.

The money is being raised for Bury's Riverwalk

School for handicapped children.

Pictured here are, from left, Clare (8), Sharon (9), Kelly (5) and Lindsay (8), with Studios Cinema manager, Mr Pat Church (Free Press picture).

At the end of our first year under the Cannon Banner, it was conference time once again and this year was to be something special. The directors of the company wanted to invite us all to their homeland, Israel. It was going to be their way of thanking us for all the hard work everyone had contributed, to help Cannon cinemas become a recognised force on the UK cinema scene. Furthermore, for the very first time, they would be inviting three lucky projectionists who, in the company's opinion, had proved to have given an outstanding work ethic over the past year. Frank was to be one of the chosen three and I was so pleased that all of his hard work had finally been recognised.

The Israel conference was a week I will never forget. It wasn't really a conference but a week's sightseeing holiday with daily trips out visiting places I had only ever seen on screen. On the very first day, we had a short tour of Tel Aviv, where we would be staying, at the Hilton Hotel, no less. The tour culminated in a look around the two main cinemas. The Shahaff Cinema was where we would be viewing some films during our stay.

A trip to Jerusalem was our first experience of being out of the main city. After this, on consecutive days we visited The Massada mountain range, the Dead Sea with Jordan in the distance, the extraordinary cable car ride up to King Herod's City on top of a mountain and also a special viewing of the Cannon film studios which, although still under construction, were in use. However, unfortunately, on the day we visited there was no filming going on. The highlight of the week for me was the trip to the Ramat David Air Force Base.

Israel

The Hilton Hotel   *The Shahaff Cinema*

Jerusalem   *Massada Mountain Range*

Cable car ride to king herod's city

Each day concluded with a banquet-style dinner at the Hilton Hotel, during which, one of the more senior executives would go over the day's events and touch upon some of the more amusing happenings, or unfortunate mishaps much to the embarrassment of the unlucky participants. We would also get a rundown on the next day's agenda.

On one evening, the senior technical engineer was doing his speech when from the rostrum he singled out our Frank and began telling everyone just why he had been chosen to be here by keeping the show alive, jokingly saying that he had worn out his projectors. He then went into great detail about the major part Frank had played in upgrading the cinema, and as a reward for all this hard work and effort, his projection room had been allocated the funding for some (as he put it) brand spanking new equipment for him to play with!

Back in our room later that evening, I don't think he stopped talking about it. In fact, I'm sure he never even slept that night; I think that was the very first time he had ever been publicly acknowledged for all his years of work and dedication to the job.

Cannon's top gun

BURY St Edmunds Cannon Cinema manger Pat Church had the surprise and delight of his life while at his firm's conference in Israel recently.

Pat was named Cannon Cinema Manager of the Year on the final night.

"It was an absolute shock," he said back in his office. "I don't regard this as just an award for me but recognition of how hard everyone involved with the cinema in Bury works to make it a success."

This year has seen business increase dramatically at the cinema, a factor which has led to the town being considered for a new super-cinema investment.

As well as a personalised trophy and a certifcate marking Pat's achievement, he has also won a £500 holiday for himself, wife Geraldine and son Stuart, 14.

Pat's starring role ... Pat Church with his Cannon Cinema Manager of the Year certificate and trophy.

The culmination of this magnificent conference was, the Gala dinner night where I received the coveted award of 'Manager of the Year'. Both Frank and I had succeeded in making sure that they wouldn't be forgetting the name 'Bury St Edmunds' in the foreseeable future, but after all the glamour, excitement and recognition, all we wanted to do was to get home to our families.

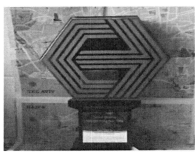

The Local Press Coverage and The Award Itself

My Son Made This Banner Whilst We Journeyed Home

Back home, and once all of the excitement had subsided, it was back to business. We now really did have something to work up to. The press had latched onto the award announcement and now wanted to support us in any future campaigns.

Frank was busy preparing for his new equipment that was going to be imminent, and it was going to consist of the latest non-rewind platters that would carry a full programme. This meant the film would be fed out to the projector from the centre of the reel which would lay flat on a plate, no more spools or 'Tower' systems for us. This piece of equipment was commonly known as a cake-stand due to its minor resemblance to the real article, and of course a modern looking update on Frank's worn out projectors.

The day soon arrived for the installation, and Frank was like all his Christmases and birthdays had rolled into one. It was so pleasing just to see him joyously working alongside the engineers.

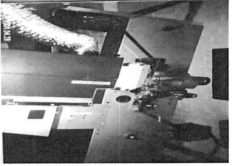

Over the next five years we flourished very nicely, feeding off our earlier successes with the company. The quality of film release was at a peak for the era and cinema had now become 'The place to be'.

I now had a fulltime assistant and a very content projection team, so that meant I could have some regular domestic life away from work, something that had been done in fits and starts over so many important years. My son, Stuart, had grown up so fast and I felt his childhood years had passed me by. As I mentioned earlier, his time with the Cathedral Choir was something I felt I missed out on as I could never seem to get to any of the events, he was performing in. I would cover for Gerry so as she and her mother could attend. They never missed one and I would get a blow by blow account later on. Gerry always said his solo moments never failed to reduce her to tears. I would have given everything to be there if I could. His proudest moment with the Cathedral Choir was to attend a music festival at a cathedral in Amsterdam.

Once his voice broke and he could no longer attain the high notes required of a chorister, he still continued with his interest in music. He caused both myself and his mother quite a shock when he said he had joined the Glen Morriston Pipe Band. Bagpipes? He loved the experience, but I dread to think just what the neighbours thought of him practising in our living room. His two best friends from school, Nathaniel and Gavin, had similar interests in music and they would all spend many hours whilst Gerry and I were working, writing and performing music which, again I'm sure, must have caused our neighbours a few headaches. I bet the volume was at full blast, but they never complained; in fact, quite the opposite. They said that they would switch everything off just to listen to them. They became more and more proficient and Gerry and I were planning our 25th wedding anniversary shin-dig, so we asked them to provide the entertainment for the first part of the evening. That certainly spurred them on into becoming Stu Nat and Gav (SNAG). A job well done, but what to do for the rest of the evening?

We managed to secure the services of Gerry's favourite Irish entertainer, Brendan Shine, for the evening and what a day we had.

It was occasions such as this that made the workload so much more bearable as it was always a juggling act running a cinema, sometimes weeks on end, without a break and keeping a stable home life. I always considered myself very lucky that every member of my close family supported me without any reservations whatsoever.

Stuart was by now in his final years of schooling and every chance he got he would be in the cinema, wanting to do odd jobs to help out and became another honorary member of our young floor staff. After some contemplation, I decided that he could join the team on an official basis for a couple of weekend shifts and he was in his element. For the next three years life seemed so good to us.

Once leaving school, he was, like so many other teenagers, unsure as to what he wanted to do with his life. Two choices seemed certain, cinema or music. At the time there were no long term opportunities in the area for cinema work, so he decided to pursue an advert he had come across for an entertainer at Pontins

Holiday Camp, Weston-Super-Mare. They were holding auditions not too far away, so off he went and, on the strength of it, he was offered a position.

Excited, apprehensive and the fear of the unknown, all mingled together in his mind as plans were being made. It meant the choir and the band had to go and we know that upset him greatly. Still the days ticked on and we prepared for our son to leave home for pastures new.

The day arrived and we took him to the railway station. With all the instructions he needed, we waved him goodbye with the knowledge we were only a phone call away. We had a tearful journey home; his mother knowing that he had flown the coop. After a couple of hours, we both were coming to terms with the emptiness and quiet within the house when suddenly the telephone burst into life. "I'm in London waiting for the next train back home," Stuart said on the phone. He just couldn't do it, and to tell the truth, neither Gerry or me were all that surprised, but we were back on that station platform to welcome him back as if he'd been gone for ages.

It seemed that Stuart's desire was to follow my footsteps and try and make a career in the cinema business.

During the same week I got to speak of this with my area manager, who said, "Leave it to me and I will see what I can do. If he really wants to be in cinema, I'm sure we can find something for him."

A week later, Stuart received a letter explaining that there was a vacancy for a trainee manager at the Cannon Cinema, Northampton. Would he be interested?

It was like a whirlwind getting him there to meet Brian Wrathall, a manager I knew very well from all our previous meetings and functions. As I expected, they hit it off right from the start. There would be a flat he could share with another new staff member and of course he wasn't going to be too far from home.

Stuart At Northampton

Chapter Ten
M.G.M Cinemas 1992–1995

Six months later, it was noticeable that business administration with Cannon seemed to have gone into meltdown. We were operating so differently from the vibrant days of a few years past and it didn't really come as any surprise to be notified that the company had been sold out to the MGM group.

It was a time of great uncertainty as MGM only seemed to want large city-centre cinemas. We were told we would all still operate under the Cannon Banner until final decisions had been made. Little did we know then, but this would go on for months and make us all unsure of what the future held.

In 1992, I was given a party and presented with a framed certificate for completing 25 year service, all set out in the MGM format, and here we were still operating as a Cannon cinema. It was also noticeable that many smaller cinemas were disappearing. In fear that we might go the same way, myself and the current team produced our very own promotional video, extolling the virtues of a smaller site. This obviously must have had some impact because within a few weeks we were informed that we would become an MGM Cinema.

We all felt very fortunate as the fabric of the cinema was upgraded to present the MGM-required image and the staff were all kitted out in their new livery. In return, we did everything possible to promote our new identity, to the extent of having an official name change ceremony with the mayor to officiate the unveiling of our new name plaque in the entrance foyer.

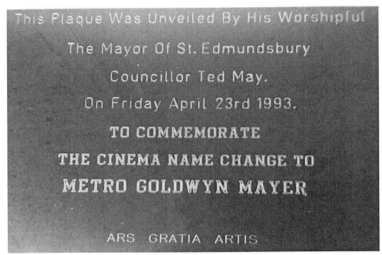

This Plaque Was Unveiled By His Worshipful
The Mayor Of St. Edmundsbury
Councillor Ted May.
On Friday April 23rd 1993.
TO COMMEMORATE
THE CINEMA NAME CHANGE TO
METRO GOLDWYN MAYER

ARS GRATIA ARTIS

Before I knew it, another year had passed by. and I found out that the old Cannon cinema in Northampton was going to be closed and boarded up as MGM were opening their purpose-built nine-screen multiplex cinema. This left our Stuart with a dilemma, what to do now? Don't ask me why but MGM came up trumps and transferred him back home as a temporary trainee manager until a new position could be found.

For the next few months, it really did become a family business. Whilst he was back in Bury, he passed his driving test and was now mobile and ready for his next move.

As it turned out, his next move was not too long in coming and he was promoted to assistant manager at the newly opened six-screen multiplex cinema in Bedford.

Sadly, the reign of MGM was very short-lived and only lasted four years. During that time, we did pick up a couple of awards, as in 1992 I completed my 25th year here at this cinema and MGM presented me with a certificate entitled 'Award for Loyal Service', then the following year I was a runner up in their 'Good Management Scheme'.

Once again, we all felt very confident in moving forward with, yet again, the new owners and could present them with visual proof of our previous endeavours in promoting the past three companies with the promise of repeating that loyalty to them. Now it was just a matter of waiting to hear who our new operators would be. Whilst this lull in the proceedings seemed to have put us all in limbo, Stuart was by now very nicely settled in Bedford, and one day informed us that he had been seeing a girl and would like to bring her home to meet us. A mutual date, and a time was set up, when I knew work would not require my attention. Gerry and I waited anxiously for their arrival, and once the initial introductions were over, all the apprehension on both sides just faded away and it was fun and laughter all the way. Shelley instantly became an extension to the family. It was moments like this that made all the pressure of work more bearable as I cherished these special family moments that seemed to pass one by so quickly.

Shortly after this, Stuart and Shelley announced their engagement. Here was my boy, suddenly a young man, planning to get married.

Chapter Eleven
Virgin Cinemas 1995–1995

What a strange year this turned out to be as the entire MGM cinema operation in the UK was bought out by Sir Richard Branson's Virgin group. They only wanted a certain mix from the cinema stock and subsequently sold off 90 of the smallest cinemas to Cinven, an international private equity firm and the newly formed ABC Cinemas, headed by Barry Jenkins, the managing director of the now-defunct Cannon company. He had had the foresight to buy the ABC brand name when Cannon had bought them out several years earlier, and I believe he always had the intention of re-creating the well-established ABC circuit, albeit on a much lesser scale.

Virgin wanted to concentrate on converting the larger sites into multiplexes. The original deal was for ABC to acquire 30 cinemas, but they actually ended up taking on 90 which in retrospect put so much pressure on this new company from the word go.

For us it meant another change of ownership, not that it altered anything as we had no dealings with Virgin, not even a name change. We continued to trade under the now-defunct MGM banner until a new future was mapped out for us.

A B C Cinemas 1995–1999

Barry Jenkins established himself as managing director and his forward-thinking vision brought back to the high streets, the ABC name that had been absent from the UK for the past ten years.

Once all the Virgin and MGM problems had been put to bed, the newly formed company forged ahead with renewed vigour. It reminded me of the old Cannon days, but I suppose it would as mostly all the head office staff were ex Cannon personnel, just like Barry Jenkins. For us out in the field, it really was a case of Deja vu and all the good times with Cannon came flooding back.

Once again, we put all our endeavours into promoting the ABC name to the town.

Toys steal a march on box office stars

THE TOYS ARE BACK IN TOWN Siobhan Gallagher two, with dad John from Stanton, meeting a giant Buzz Lightyear (left) and Woody the cowboy when manager Pat Church welcome them to the ABC cinema in Bury

Home front was still being juggled with all the different work upheavals, and Stuart and Shelley's wedding preparations were in full flow. Both Gerry and I were over the moon for both of them and the day couldn't come quick enough. However, I was in so much turmoil and torment with the change of companies and all of the added pressure, that it may have seemed that I was less interested. Nothing could have been further from the truth and here I was again walking a fine line between work and family. Fortunately for me, Gerry took the helm, just like she had on so many occasions. She kept me updated on a regular basis and once a date had been set, I managed to arrange some away time.

I wouldn't have missed it for the world and it turned out to be one of the proudest days of my life, watching my lad become a married man. Not only that, but I had now gained a daughter.

Stuart and Shelley on their Wedding Day

For the first couple of years, it was all systems go. The company was in a buoyant mood and many of the head office faces were a blast from the past, but it soon became clear that following all the initial bursts of energy and enthusiasm, it was beginning to dwindle, I could recognise the signs.

It was also about this time we got to find out Shelley was expecting. 'I'm gonna be a Grandad'. There was so much to take in and with everything that was happening at the cinema, that juggling act syndrome took over again. The next eight months passed without me even noticing, but right on cue out popped our little Ryan.

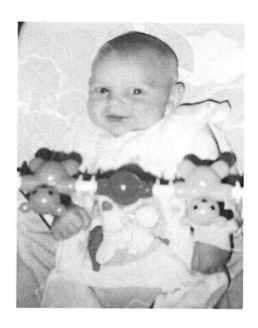

Ryan, our first Grandchild

Just as I had predicted, it was announced that ABC were running into financial difficulties. The '90' cinemas deal had overstretched everything they had envisaged. Most of these cinemas were large city centre sites that were old and expensive to run and maintain, large city centre stock. The multiplex phenomenon was in full swing and was having a marked effect on the high street. Many of the traditional cinemas were slowly disappearing, but we managed to trundle on, despite there being some very dark days.

We were never sure what next week would bring forth, but it was obvious to us all that something would have to give, just a matter of what and when. All the head office staff that still remained were putting on a brave face and trying so hard to keep the general morale up, come what may, but after much speculation, it came as no surprise that ABC were selling out to Odeon.

Now, for many people, the name Odeon means The Rank Organisation e.g. 'The man with the Gong!', but this was a whole new ball game. The company had been re-styled into the futuristic world of computerised methods of cinema management, a completely new and daunting phase in this cinema's history, and as ABC bowed out, it became very clear just what Odeon had in store for us:

Myself personally had some very difficult times with Odeon and at times nearly called it a day! (As detailed in my first book, *The Smallest Show on Earth*).

Again, whilst all this turmoil was going on, we seemed to spend as much away time as possible nipping over to Bedford for more treasured family moments. On one such visit we were told that another addition was on the way.

Chapter Twelve
Odeon 1999–2005

From the very first day when I had to meet a contingency of Odeon personnel, it became obvious that they just didn't know what to do with two small cinemas that shared a building with a bingo hall. This was something that just didn't fit into their portfolio. They thoroughly scrutinised all we had to offer and then left the building to have a meeting at a nearby hotel, informing me that they would be back later to give me an overview on our future. It was a very strange day, and a very unsettling one for all the staff as we were still trading as ABC despite all the daily accounts now going to Odeon head office.

About five hours later, part of the group returned and laid out what decisions they had agreed upon. The main overriding factor was that we were the only cinema outlet in the county, and to turn their back on us would look very bad on Odeon as a whole and threaten the possibility of gathering some very negative press reviews. The overall view was that they would take us on for a short term whilst the development of a new multiplex cinema in the town was decided upon. This proposed development was in the very early planning stages and was, at the very least, a couple of years away from being finalised.

Over the next few weeks, there was a flurry of activity as all the old ABC furniture and fittings were replaced with Odeon-style signage and I thought to myself, *Here we go again!*

During all this activity and turmoil, our second grandchild duly put in an appearance. Another little boy, Cameron. So many lovely family times lay ahead, of which no one will ever realise just what a welcome release those days were from the problems that Odeon was causing us.

Cameron, our second grandson

As expected, and something I had been warned about, I was summoned to a meeting at Odeon's London offices and what a mind-numbing day it turned out to be. I also noted just how few of us there were, only to find out that Odeon had decreed a mass cinema closure or sell off. This included most of the old ABC sites plus some of their own underperforming sites. This resulted in a mass redundancy programme being put in place and the company's statement to this was a 'streamlining operation'.

The entire afternoon was taken up with different training sessions on the new computerised systems that where being installed as soon as we returned to our own sites. Looking around the room I could see the many puzzled faces along with mine. This was something so very different to anything we had previously experienced, and to have it all thrust upon us in one mind blowing afternoon was quite overwhelming. At the end of that session it was made very clear we should embrace it and learn. Anyone who couldn't, or wouldn't, well resignations would be accepted. It suddenly became very clear that comrades and such were now a thing of the past. It was all going to be hi-tech and impersonal from now on.

Back home, work was well underway on transforming the cinema frontage and foyer, something that, by now, we had become quite used to. It was just a matter of removing the now obsolete ABC internal fittings and colour schemes and replacing them with something different so as to give it a new look of Odeon. Newly installed was the box office computerised ticketing system and a ticket collection point along with all the office computer systems that were directly linked to the London offices and overseen by the IT team there. The only good thing was that they agreed to upgrade some of the inner fabric as well as the frontage.

It was a very trying time, training staff that had no previous computer knowledge, as even I was struggling to remember everything. Luckily, the younger members of staff at that time were a bonus and always appeared more knowledgeable than some of us on the intricacies of certain aspects. Together, we got through it, and embraced it, to a certain extent.

During our next little staff get together, after patting ourselves on the back, it was decided that, as with all the companies before, we would do the same again and do our best to promote the name Odeon to the town.

Pictures of happiness!

81

With our many welcoming foyer displays and the odd press review on our endeavours, we fared very nicely as did our business levels. The hardest challenge was keeping top side of the 'blasted computers', but as I've said before, "You learn from your mistakes," and I certainly did.

I always dreaded the phone ringing and it being the IT department with a query. They always spoke so fast in a jargon that was a completely foreign language to me. "You should have done this!" or "You should have pressed that!" A five-minute call would see me hang up the phone, my mind a complete blur.

I have always maintained you can only be as good as the support around you, and 18 months later, no one was more surprised than me when after a general company meeting in London, following the evening meal, our cinema was singled out to receive the coveted award, aptly named 'Odeon Oscars'. The next day, back on site, we proudly put it on display for all to see as it was a complete team effort.

I have always felt blessed in having the best around me, and every time a company recognised this, be it a team effort or a particular staff member achievement, it always highlighted that feeling. This was the case when they presented a 25-year service award to my very own 'partner in crime'.

We had now been under the Odeon banner for just over three years, and during that time, the cinema in Bedford where Stuart was based, had been taken over by a new exhibitor on the block, Cineworld! During our regular telephone conversations, he was challenging the fact that he was not sure if he could conform to their work ethics. I could sense the dissolution in his tone as he had been trained in the traditional ideology that customer care is paramount to the job. In the middle of all this uncertainty, he also casually announced that Shelley was expecting again…what???

Despite it being a very testing and trying time working for a company that didn't really want to be here, the time flew by. Then came the announcement that the first foundations had been dug for the up and coming multiplex development which would be operated by Cineworld. That's when the truth really dawned on me. Nearly everyone I met out and about asked the same thing, "What are you going to do when Cineworld opens? It'll be the end of you!"

This went on for weeks and my staff were becoming quite despondent as they were being asked the same questions. I could offer no clear vision of a future, only a pipe dream! Frank then dropped his bombshell and told me he had decided to retire. His general health was causing a few concerns both here and at home, and after the initial shock of his statement, we all knew it was the right decision for his wellbeing.

We had a little staff get together to mark the occasion and say our different fond farewells. It truly was the end of an era in more ways than one. Frank was the one person I would truly miss as he had been my right hand in dealing with the many technical problems over recent years and now it was back to the good ole bad old days. However, I need not have worried, as the assistant projectionist, Ian, was immediately promoted to 'chief' and proved a worthy successor.

Then right on cue, the next addition to our family came on the scene. This time, a granddaughter, Georgia.

Georgia our Granddaughter

Over the years we have had so much fun and laughter together. It makes everything so worthwhile, and even though she is now the age of 18, we can never wait to get together again and cause mayhem wherever we are. It doesn't get any better than this.

Shortly after Georgia's birth, Stuart decided to try another direction in the work ethic, but although the love of film and cinema would never leave him, being a dedicated family-man, he could see it was the right thing to do. With a new direction in place, one could clearly see his outward demeanour flourish.

A few months later, I had a telephone call from the owner of the property and our landlord, Norman Jacobs, based at Wisbech. This was a man I had known for many years due to his avid interest and enthusiasm in cinemas of which he had several under his ownership, all leased out to various operators. We had a mutual liking for each other and during our lengthy conversation, it turned out Odeon had approached him with the intention of renewing the lease, so as to keep control of the property after the opening of the new Cineworld multiplex which was about six months away from completion. It transpired that a deal had been struck between the two companies to close our doors the very same day the multiplex opened, and board up the cinema side of the building until another use could be found. This meant that whilst Odeon held the lease, they could ensure it couldn't be used as a cinema again and Cineworld would have no opposition. Apparently, this was something they both did for each other so as to control the exhibition side of the business. Odeon would close, what they deemed as their lesser operations, and in return Cineworld would not infringe on Odeon's prime sites.

As I said, Norman Jacobs was a cinema man and he saw through this ruse immediately. In the subsequent weeks, he was a great help in paving the way for discussions with Mr Trevor Wicks, another great cinema enthusiast, who also leased some property off of Norman.

Trevor had branched out with his own little independent cinema empire across Norfolk which he had aptly named 'Hollywood Cinemas'. His 'flagship' site was the old Odeon Cinema which he had taken on after its closure in Anglia Square Norwich. Luckily for us, I knew Trevor from back in the old ABC days. A deal was struck between himself and Norman Jacobs to bring us into his little empire after the demise of Odeon, so with great anticipation we formulated plans and a strategy so as to continue the business once Odeon bowed out.

Our landlord, true to his word, made sure that Odeon rigorously stuck to the terms of the lease and could only remove what was directly theirs such as the signage and computer systems etc. All the furniture and fittings had to stay on site, despite Odeon's request that they had spent a considerable sum to upgrade these items and could use them elsewhere. As far as they were aware, the building was going to be put in mothballs and sealed up. However, much to their annoyance, Norman stood firm.

So, whilst Odeon was busy winding us down, all the things we would need to replace what was being removed was secretly being stored away until required.

Time ticked around and on Thursday, 9 November 2005, we closed the building. Teams of different people were drafted in to start the dismantling of all the Front of House signs and then the interior ones. I remember thinking to myself, *Be careful, we shall need to re-use that space.* They were just ripping things off walls and chopping cables whilst another team were busy taking out the computer systems and removing all my files from the office area.

Around lunchtime, the staff started to appear as requested to collect anything personal they had on site and receive their redundancy notices and a goodbye from the area manager. I think their buoyant mood rather perplexed him; little did he know! Shortly after, Norman put in an appearance to check over his building with the Odeon head office and legal team. Once that was out of the way, they then performed the official switch off and the building plunged into darkness; doors locked and bolted and with all keys handed to the landlord, they duly departed.

After a quick cordial chat, Norman wished me all the luck in the world with the parting words, "Keep in touch," as he handed the keys back over to me, and from that point on it was all systems go.

Chapter Thirteen
Hollywood Cinemas 2005–2010

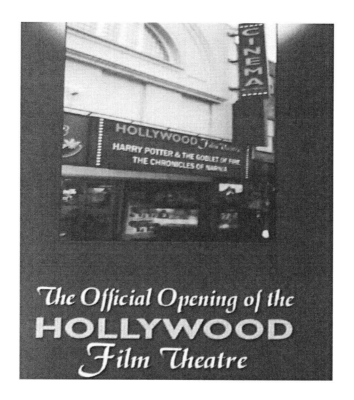

Later, that very same day, most of the staff plus a few drafted in workmen arrived, on cue, to start the process of repairing the damage after the Odeon strip out and putting in place all the new look signage. Tomorrow was going to be a brand new start.

During the evening, as the new stock started to arrive, the mood of everyone was so upbeat that one would think it was party time, and why not.

My only disappointment was that the local press showed very little interest in the fact that we were still open for business. The main emphasis was on the new eight-screen multiplex, the future look of Bury St Edmunds. Such was the might of their marketing department and input from the local councillors who needed to protect their incentives in getting this new complex into town.

We still had our loyal customers as always, and we all knew we just had to ride out this new wave of cinemagoing until the novelty wore off. We embarked on our own limited campaign with all the local businesses that had mutually supported us throughout the years and slowly and quietly got the message over that we were open for business as usual.

Over the next couple of years, we struggled on, business being very mediocre to say the least and Hollywood had to bail us out on several occasions, something I always felt guilty about. We always knew it was going to be tough trading against brand new opposition, and at times I felt that we had let Trevor Wicks down, with him being our saviour not so long ago. The might and film-booking power of Cineworld stopped us from picking up on the new releases we needed to screen. We were, however, a thorn in their side as, in their eyes, we were not supposed to be trading.

During the winter months of 2008 we decided to curtail our opening hours so as to reduce the running costs during this expensive period. This allowed us to soldier on, but we could find no definitive answers to the onslaught and business tactics of Cineworld. Most months we didn't even meet our monthly expenditure.

Then, one fateful day (a day I had been secretly dreading), I was called to a meeting with Hollywood and their accountants at their main branch in Norwich. The long and short of it was that we could not be allowed to go on any longer. We had all given it our best shot but we were becoming a liability on Hollywood. As a small independent group, they could no longer support us and to that end we would have to close our doors at the end of the next trading week. My job was to return and prepare for the inevitable close down.

With a heavy heart, I broke the news to the few staff that remained and informed all our business contacts. The press got hold of it and it seemed to make their day. Don't they just love bad news?

THE END

Oldest cinema in town to close after 80 years

THE Hollywood Film Theatre, in Hatter Street, Bury St Edmunds, is set to close next week. The oldest cinema in town will

by Jo Thewlis

Cinema's last picture show

Curtain falls on town cinema

THE end of an era was signalled last night when the doors of Hollywood Film Theatre, in Bury St Edmunds, were finally closed.

Pat Church, manager of the cinema in Hatter Street for the past 42 years, turned the key in the lock for the last time after owners Hollywood Cinemas pulled out of the venture.

Mr Church, 61, said: "The public's response has been overwhelming, it has really shocked me.

"People have grown up with this cinema – it's part of their lives."

The final film also marked the redundancy of seven staff at the picture house, which has been running on the site since 1924.

But Mr Church is in talks with other independent chains to discuss re-opening the operation, with the possibility of turning it into an art house cinema.

He said: "The staff are mightily upset but, hopefully, something will come along.

"This place means everything to me."

Pat's wife Geraldine has worked at the cinema for 35 years and said letters, cards and phone calls from well wishers had been pouring in since news of the closure spread.

Mrs Church, 62, said: "A lot of people are still in shock, this place is an institution.

"This place is Pat's job, his world.

It has been his whole life."

Hollywood Cinemas' lease of the building from owner Norman Jacobs MBE runs until November this year, so Mr Church has a few months to attract a new owner.

Anyone interested in taking the cinema on or offering their support can contact Mr Church on 01284 762586.

■ See Letters Page 14.

HIS WORLD: Cinema manager Pat Church

During our final week I wrote a series of letters to as many independent operators as I could come up with, offering the lease and our services as an addition to their businesses. I received several replies, but our balance sheets of the past three years were against us from the onset. However, promising interest was shown from Picturehouse Cinemas, a predominately Art House circuit. They operated an ex Cannon / ABC site in Cambridge. I had often studied their programme content and operating format with wishful thinking, but every time I approached Hollywood with a change of direction, it fell on deaf ears. It was so alien from their own operation mandate.

A week later, an onsite meeting was arranged with one of the Picturehouse directors, Mrs Lyn Goleby, just to look over the cinema and see just what we had to offer.

As I sat in my office, which was now situated within this cold, dark and very lonely place, I pondered just how to sell the hidden potential that I knew laid within to a same-minded company. It had always been a dream of mine since the introduction of the multiplex to give an alternative venue, in keeping with the ambience of the historic core of Bury St Edmunds.

From the very onset of that meeting there appeared to be a joining of minds, and future ideas were mapped out for the re-invention of our cinema. The only blot on the landscape was that they couldn't possibly enter into negotiations for at least another six months or more, but felt very confident that we would be able to move forward as a Picturehouse venue. With that said, the meeting ended, but it was on the understanding that we would have regular contact and progress reports.

I cannot begin to describe just how elated and excited I felt as Lyn left the building. Anyone who knows me will always recognise my legendary film title quotes to every situation throughout my life; today it was Virginia McKenna in *Carve Her name With Pride*. To this day, that's how I always view Lyn Goleby.

My next dilemma was to determine what we could do for the next six or more months. We just couldn't lay idle and shut, that would be defeatist. I got together the now depleted team and we formulated a plan.

If Hollywood could be persuaded to re-open us on a much lesser scale and with a skeleton staff, all taking a reduction in pay but with a monthly bonus based on whatever profit we made (if any), then we could continue trading until Picturehouse could take us on. I set up a meeting with Trevor from Hollywood, and his accountants, and after a lot of discussion it was agreed that as there would be no capital outlay in re-opening. Everyone was in favour of the new working practices put forward. We could reopen for the interim period, but with one proviso put in place. This was that we would not be known as Hollywood Film Theatre. We would have to operate separately from the rest of the group. There would be no cost involved in name changing and we would merely operate as 'Hollywood Cinema'. That was fine by me. We were going to open again; that was all that mattered. After so many name changes over the years, one more wouldn't hurt. It was time to get back out there and 'bang the drum'. We were Back!!!

My first job was to notify all the different press sources that we were going to re-open. What a disappointment that turned out to be. They just didn't seem interested, though they had made a big enough splash when we were forced to close. The press coverage of our re-opening consisted of one single column on page three.

Hollywood celebrates reprieve

THE Hollywood Film Theatre, in Bury St Edmunds, will re-open next week after a rescue package was negotiated with the existing owners.

Hollywood Cinemas have agreed to keep the film house in Hatter Street open throughout the summer season, until their lease expires in November.

Pat Church, manager of the cinema for the past 42 years, said: "This is a great weight off my mind.

"There was such an overwhelming public response, they couldn't really refuse us."

The oldest picture house in Bury closed three weeks ago amid concern from film fans, who had affection for the cinema which opened in 1924.

But thanks to public support, Mr Church has negotiated a stay of execution to give him time to find new backers to run the business.

Mr Church said: "I'll be very pleased to open the doors again.

"It has been quite humbling to think what the cinema means to people."

The picture house will open its doors next Friday, but will now be known as Hollywood Cinema rather than the Hollywood Film Theatre.

Trevor Wicks, director of Hollywood Cinemas, said: "We are extremely pleased we have managed to re-open the cinema so quickly.

"We are very pleased with the support we have received and look forward to working together to secure the future of the cinema."

Once up and running again, it was heart-warming to get so many complimentary comments from the public. The shock of all those closing headlines had made a lot of people sit up and realise 'you don't know what you have, until it's gone'. Some of our customers hadn't even realised we had closed and re-opened.

All of a sudden, once we had re-opened and got ourselves established again, we noticed a slight upsurge in our admission levels and could also sense that some people were trickling back to us after becoming disillusioned with Cineworld. This made my monthly communication with Lyn Goleby much more interesting. If we could just keep this operation going, there would be light at the end of our very long dark tunnel.

The tunnel turned out to be longer than expected as six months turned out to be a year, but in 2010, as promised, Picturehouse arrived in Bury St Edmunds.

Chapter Fourteen
Picturehouse 2010–2012

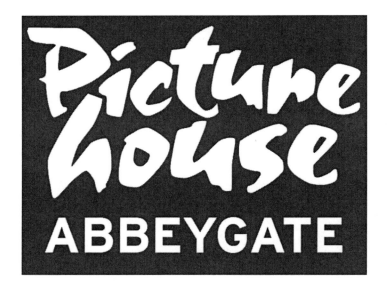

My very first hurdle to overcome with this new company was the name. Picturehouse, as a common policy, named all of their cinemas by the town name followed by the word Picturehouse. Knowing how all the locals had shortened the town name from Bury St Edmunds, I knew we would locally become 'Bury Picturehouse' regardless of what was on the signage. The thought of that filled me with dread, plus I always had this dream of bringing back the name 'Abbeygate'.

The name Abbeygate was synonymous as the cinema's location was linked to Abbeygate Street, The Abbey Gateway and the Abbey Gardens.

We had several heated arguments on the subject and it was finally agreed that the public should vote for the name. A press release went out inviting the public to give their views on the subject. As I expected, the name 'Abbeygate Cinema' prevailed, but as a compromise I had to agree to having the company name as the main heading and so we became Picturehouse Abbeygate. I could live with that.

True to her word, now nearly a year ago, plans were immediately drawn up to completely re-design both auditoriums to a very high standard, and once completed, this would locally be known as the 'WOW' factor. The front entrance and foyer were just being tidied up as negotiations were taking place for a takeover of the now vacant part of the same property next door. If successful, it would mean a new entrance.

In return for enduring the inconvenience of all the works going on, we gave consent for Winners Bingo, who shared the frontage plus the rear of the property, to have their signage put in a prominent position. Negotiations went in our favour and, once finalised and the architects had completed their brief, more construction work was forthcoming.

Our new look Screen One   *Seats and sofas,*

Screen Two   *A nice cosy ambience*

Temporary Entrance

Along with the auditorium re-modelling, the very same thing was happening up in the projection department. The age of 35mm film and a resident projectionist was being replaced with the state of the art Digital Computerised and Satellite systems. This new technology would enable us to screen live events from around the world. Imagine an Opera or a ballet or Play being performed LIVE the other side of the world, beamed via satellite direct to the projector.

This was going to open up for us a brand new market. We were certainly changing, at a pace.

A Digital Projector

Satellite Transmitter   *Receiving Dish*

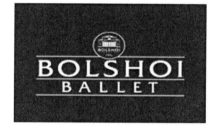

National Theatre Live

All the recent activity had created so much public interest and curiosity to see just what had been done within the cinema that our business levels took off and the live event screenings created a whole new audience. After spending the past few years in the wilderness, fighting for survival, we suddenly found ourselves on top of the game and revelled in our new found success that looked to keep on building.

However, it was not always as straight forward as one would expect. In the early days, transmission signals were a nightmare depending on which part of the world the production was being transmitted from. The Bolshoi ballet, direct from Moscow, was always one of our biggest headaches and of course the picture output from the projector was only as good as the input signal. At times we could only stand there helpless as it was controlled by alien forces so to speak. I do well remember one time when we were tuning in, ready for screening, and whatever we did there was just no signal coming through. The National helpline was of no use whatsoever, with a full house down below eagerly waiting for that night's Live Opera. We rang another of our cinemas doing the same thing, only to find out that everything was fine there. This meant it must be a fault in our equipment. "What do we do now?" Don't ask me why, but a thought suddenly occurred to me that maybe the satellite dish had moved off line, most unlikely as it was locked on, but with this in mind I cautiously made my way across a snow-covered flat roof to the dish, and lo and behold; upon inspection the entire dish was covered in hard-packed snow and ice. So, in full evening dress, freezing my doofahs off, there I was scraping clean the receiver dish. Thereafter, the signal came through at full strength. Now you know the lengths that we go to ensure 'The show must go on!'

It was now 2012 and I was reminded that this would be my 50th year in the cinema industry, 46 of those years being here in Bury St Edmunds. Where had that time gone; I had just been doing my job, but my, the years had flown by.

I was told in no uncertain terms that we could not let this milestone pass by unnoticed. So, for the next few weeks I was asked to keep out of the way whilst the staff arranged a little celebration party. Who was I to argue?

The only thing that was expected of me was to choose my favourite film, as after the party celebrations, all the invited guests would be asked to join me and watch a film! I had seen thousands of films over the years. Did I really have a favourite?

It was also around this time that I was in the process of writing my first ever book which I had entitled after a film which I was now proud to call 'my most favourite film', *The Smallest Show on Earth*.

The scene was set and what a night it turned out to be. There were so many surprise guests from years past and there were gifts galore, the most fascinating one being a special magnum of champagne from 20th Century Fox (how on earth had they got wind of this? I guess I will never know). Anyway, let the party commence:

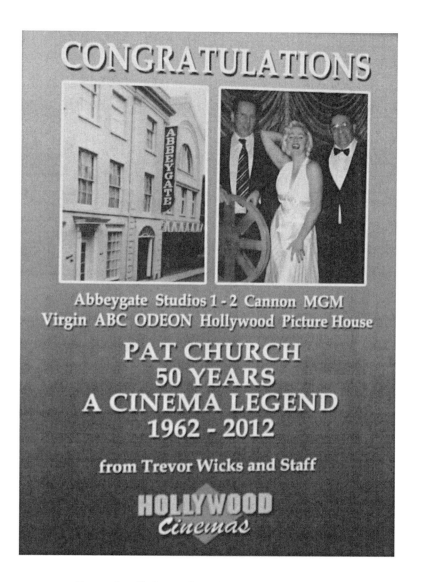

Framed wall plaque from the ex-Hollywood gang

*Carraige Clock from
the Abbeygate team.*

*My cake Celebrating 50
years in the industry*

*The surprise Champagne
from 20th Century Fox*

The follow up to this event was the press coverage which caused quite a stir when it was published. So many people called into the cinema wanting to say congratulations or just to have a friendly chat with me about the cinema.

A couple of months after this, the council wanted to do something special to mark the event and commissioned a decorated street bollard which stands not too far from the cinema. Will I ever get back to normal?

The press that followed the party

The Street bollard that suddenly appeared

Whilst all of this was going on, work started on the vacant part of the building to transform it into a delicatessen-style kiosk, restaurant and bar. This would mean going to the pictures would no longer be an in/out venture and that you would now be able to combine a relaxing drink or sociable bite to eat along with a good movie.

As mentioned earlier, the plans also included a new entrance to the cinema that would double up with the new area so as to create the space to introduce a lift and allow disabled access into both screens. This was something we had never been able to offer before due to the original layout of the building.

We all watched the building progress by the day, getting more and more excited as each area was completed (well I know I was), but the works seemed to go on forever. You just wouldn't imagine how difficult it was, transforming this old building into its modern guise. The upper floor was all different levels and we needed it to be wheelchair-friendly, a level playing field, so to speak. Our biggest problem was that some of the raised sections were main structures and changing these would cause serious knock on effects if disturbed. However, by introducing some ramped-up areas and a few dips to compensate, we got over the problem.

After nearly two years of planning and building, we were finally ready to introduce our new look to our patrons.

An old architectural fireplace that became my museum

Our new entrance

The next hurdle was again to come up with a name to give this shared area its own identity. Although being part of the cinema operation, after many different suggestions had been considered, an idea arose that as the entire property address had been number 4, Hatter Street (despite never being known as such once, each new business had taken on its own heading), the historic doorway had always been the Front Door to Number 4. Therefore, as this was now to become the main entrance to both cinema and restaurant, it made it somewhat unique. There would be no other restaurant called No 4.

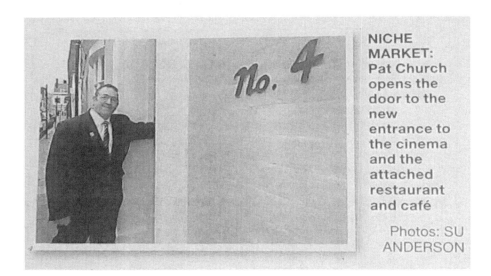

NICHE MARKET: Pat Church opens the door to the new entrance to the cinema and the attached restaurant and café

Photos: SU ANDERSON

We had all worked so hard over the past four years to get us to this position and considered we were riding on the crest of a wave, but after all this work and effort we still had stormy waters ahead that were way beyond our control.

It appeared that the Picturehouse financial backers dried up and pulled out overnight leaving them high and dry, so to speak. In an amazing twist of fate, would you believe, it was Cineworld who stepped in and bought them out lock stock and barrel.

Cineworld, it seemed, had been looking at the steady growth of this arm of the business over the past year or two, but as it was far removed from their own type of operation, buying up a well-established group was the ideal situation to now control the arthouse and mainstream product.

From a site level, nothing really changed and we continued trading as Picturehouse. However, we all knew that Cineworld was pulling the strings.

Cineworld takes over Abbeygate

Pat Church outside the Abbeygate Picturehouse

After only a few short months, the Monopolies commission picked up on this venture and decreed that Cineworld would have complete domination in certain towns and counties which would result in unfair trading. They also decreed those three sites which fell well into this category would have to be sold on, with immediate effect. These sites were Aberdeen, Bury St Edmunds and Cambridge.

Aberdeen was leased from the East Lothian Council, so this ended up being reverted back into the council's control and the cinema continued its arthouse presence in the city.

Cambridge and Bury St Edmunds, however, were a different kettle of fish. It was suggested that both sites be sold off together as a package deal and so plans were put in place for potential buyers to view both existing operations.

Over the next few months, we had several visits from different potential buyers. Some were serious to see what we had to offer, but others came just to nose around. Certain parties just wanted to stamp their own brand of operation into Bury St Edmunds, which was in complete contrast to what we had achieved with Picturehouse.

Then, at the last possible moment, Cineworld suddenly announced that they were going to 'move the goalposts' and that they had decided to keep the Picturehouse site in Cambridge and put their Multiplex operation up for sale instead. This meant that now, we were, once again, a standalone site, sink or swim on our own merits.

Once this news reached all the potential buyers, they started dropping out one by one. It appeared Cambridge was the carrot and everyone thought Bury was just not big enough to go it alone; their loss!!!

Waiting in the background during the negotiations was Lyn Goleby. co-founder of Picturehouse some 25 years earlier. She had dropped out of the scene after the Cineworld takeover, but she was the one person who had the foresight to see our true potential, and after our first meeting during the decline of Hollywood days, I would always 'carve her name with pride'.

During all of this, I personally had been bestowed several awards and accolades. Although I often felt a little guilty in receiving these, I always consoled myself in that they promoted the name Abbeygate Cinema. They also had a marked effect that failure was still no longer an option. So many people would be let down should we not succeed.

I think the big surprise was the 'Lifetime Achievement Award' given at a function of the 'We Love Bury St Edmunds society' along with the much-coveted lapel badge.

The most surreal thing would be invitations just dropping on the doormat as a complete surprise and shock. Very often I would never find out just who had originally nominated me and I was left feeling grateful, but bemused at the same time.

The biggest shock of all time will come a little later, but as you can see by the certificates, it reminds me of George Lazenby *On Her Majesty's Secret Service*, I never quite made it.

Chapter Fifteen
Abbeygate 2012–Present Day

Overnight, our fortunes changed yet again into yet more unknown territory and uncertainty about what the future would hold for us. However, Lyn Goleby's enthusiasm and drive instilled us all with so much confidence that our full support was behind her, even more so as we reverted back to the single name of Abbeygate Cinema. To me it was like a dream come true, much to the amusement of others, but overnight or so it seemed the knife was twisted again.

Cineworld/Picturehouse, with whom we had been hiring the use of the original computer systems from as an independent client, informed us that all the systems would be turned off within seven days. We had one week to organise a whole new computerised system for the entire building. This was really going to be a sink or swim operation where we had to find new IT partners to help us out, until we could get our feet.

Luckily for us, we have such an understanding and loyal customer base, and they supported us unreservedly whilst this difficult transition was taking place.

Once complete, new IT systems allowed us to move forward in all areas of the business, and we launched the brand new 'Abbeygate Cinema' website. This allowed us to keep all of our valued customers up to date with all of the latest developments of both cinema and No 4 restaurant.

A couple of years passed and on the back of our continued success, planning permission was applied for and granted – to convert the back end of the building into two additional screens and completely remodel the frontage.

Pondering the future

On a more personal front I was now well into my 69th year and the past few had taken its toll on my wellbeing.

I had developed diabetes and was constantly suffering regular migraines, mostly due to all the new IT and computerised innovations. They were becoming a constant strain, so it was mutually agreed that on my forthcoming 70th birthday, I would resign from my position of general manager and hand the operation over to my current assistant, Jonathan Carpenter. This would allow me to have a break whilst the new managerial group restructured. I could then return in a lesser capacity.

To me, it seemed like an ideal solution, but suddenly, as if from nowhere I became 70 and had to sign on that dotted line, hand over keys, files and full responsibility to Jonathan.

Personally, this was possibly the hardest challenge I had faced in all of my tumultuous years in, what I regarded as, 'my' cinema. This had always been my cinema, my operation. In my mind, over the years I had merely allowed all the operating companies to put their name on 'my' building.

Stepping down, truth be told, was much more cordial and friendly than I had ever envisaged. I was to take a three-month break and then ease myself back into a part time role, customer based, where I had so wanted to devote all of my time. No more stress from computers and technology. Looking back on it now it was all as agreed and even I, deep down, knew it was for the best.

However, once away from the business, the sudden realisation really took hold of me, and within three weeks a series of epileptic seizures took place and, shortly after, hospital followed.

I know my immediate family were devastated that this had happened and it was the last thing anyone would have expected. The seizures continued whilst I was hospitalised, but after a while stopped just as mysteriously as they had started. The diagnosis was a build-up of stress and tension over a long period of time suddenly being released, and with that I was packed off back home along with the suspension of my driving licence for a year.

Being unable to drive upset me so much. How was I going to see the family in Bedford? As always though, the family was my redeeming factor. I couldn't get to them, so they came and visited me, often! However, I felt I had lost a certain amount of my independence, and how was I ever going to able to get myself back on the Front of House duties, greeting the customers that had become my friends.

All these negative thoughts contributed to me sinking into a period of depression and despair. I must have been a pain in the backside to Gerry, who took each day in its stride and was always there for me over the next three months. Then, all of a sudden, the tide turned.

A new start and the yearning to get out from the recluse I had become. I was not allowed to drive, but that was suddenly not the end of my world. I bought myself a bicycle and started to get out and about again. In doing so I bumped into so many well-wishing patrons and I began to feel that if I didn't get myself back where I belonged, I would be letting them down. As with all important decisions, my family once again supported my every move.

Bike riding

As I mentioned earlier, whilst celebrating my 50th year in the business, I had begun to write my memoirs. During this period of recuperation, I ploughed on and completed the project. It formed part of my homemade healing process and it stopped me climbing the walls.

On one weekend, when my son and his family were home, I decided to show him the finished manuscript. He read it all, and then, with a wry smile upon his face, produced an advert for a publisher who was asking for manuscripts that they could evaluate.

After much conversation and with an arm twisted up my back, I succumbed and sent off a few pages, just to get a professional opinion. Three weeks later I received a reply asking to see more. Out of complete shock, I answered that it was nowhere near finished, expecting that to be the end of the matter. However, I received a further reply which said that, 'once finished', they would like to put it into book form and publish it for me. You could have knocked me over with a feather.

About to become a published author, and feeling better than I had felt for ages, it was time to get myself back where I truly belonged.

I'd been away from the Abbeygate for nine months now and the urge to get back was only getting stronger. I set up a meeting with Lyn Goleby and a deal was made that I would return as a semiretired, casual, Front of House manager. In other words, 'the people person'. I would be there predominately for all of the 'Live' satellite events which needed promoting to exploit their full potential.

My dear wife Geraldine, or just Gerry as most people knew her, would continue to work alongside me for these events so as to cover the intermissions with her beloved sales tray and make the evening that little more special.

It was a very cautious start with mixed feelings as the working practices had obviously changed entirely, along with all the new computerised systems. For the first few weeks I felt very awkward, but that feeling soon passed.

Feeling back where we belong

It was also about this time that my autobiography had been put into book form and published. It was entitled *The Smallest Show on Earth*. Every moment of my spare time was now taken up with press and radio interviews. There was also a feature on TV's 'Anglia News'. This led on to several book-signing sessions. I was also asked to give some cinema history talks to various clubs and organisations, which I duly performed. It seemed the ideal opportunity to promote the very reason I was back, and push forward the recently appointed marketing manager's achievements on introducing not only the forthcoming live events, but also the weekly Parent and Baby shows, designed for young mothers to meet, watch a movie and have their baby with them, with dim lights on.

I was also on hand to promote our Monday morning 'Senior' shows and the monthly showings for people suffering from that interminable disease, dementia. No one will ever know, and it is so hard to put into words, how proud I was to be a part of something that could allow these people to re-live their own glory days and to see them rocking away at the music that stirred them.

I was busier now than when I had been working full time, and I was certainly back on top of my game, so to speak. However, it was also surprising to me that so many people didn't know of all the different events that were going on in our cinema, despite all the efforts to publicise them.

We mostly used the online website or in-house leaflets to promote our events. Again, the IT computerised way of life came to the forefront, but we needed more. As I've said before, everyone seemed to believe that websites and internet was the modern way forward, yet when I was out at various clubs etc., doing talks, most of the people I met didn't have a computer, so never saw any of our advertisements.

I managed to persuade several of them to pop along when next in town and become a member of the Abbeygate Cinema. This would ensure that they would get programme details sent to them each month and just as I anticipated, over a period of time, people I had met at various talks, started drifting in to the cinema, all stopping to have a chat and then signed up to the membership. They would then encourage others to come. I've always been a firm believer of the old adage 'There's no publicity like 'word of mouth'!' Nowadays, it's an extension of their club get together and I know most of them by first name terms. To me they are no longer patrons, it's like having friends round for the show:

One of several book signing sessions

Through no fault of their own, the entire management team had been taken over by computers and although they could not see it, they had all seemed to develop tunnel vision and had very little idea of what was going on around them. Even the now dark and unmanned projection rooms were controlled from a downstairs office. I fully understood that 70 percent of the time was taken up with restaurant and bar administration, and the cinema part of the business, to some extent, had to fend for itself, but I'm pleased to say that after two years of badgering and arguing my own points of view, things improved, not quite enough for my liking, but I was hopeful that we were slowly getting there.

Having seen it all, so many times before, when two different businesses combine with a shared staff and management, one or the other has to suffer. There is a whole world of difference in doing a job because you 'have' to as opposed to doing the job because you 'want' to! This has always been a philosophy of mine and it will never change.

Chapter Sixteen

Whilst plans were being finalised for the next phase of development, out of the blue, my successor, Johnathan announced that he was moving on to pastures new and that a new 'project manager' was being installed as a temporary measure. His main priority would be to oversee the new building work that was about to get underway.

Having never worked with a 'project manager' before, I was a little apprehensive, but I need not have worried as he turned out to be a really nice, friendly guy with a great interest and background in cinema. He soon became one of the greatest assets we had had for a long time.

It was about this time that the first stage of the planned re-build was about to get off the drawing board and the builders moved in for the restructuring process. There were some early unforeseen problems that ensued once they started knocking walls and ceilings about in a much-used building of its age. The architects and builders had several headaches, the biggest of which was the discovery of asbestos wall lining. This halted works for a considerable time whilst a specialist removal team moved in to take care of it. However, progress, although very slow, was evident.

The demolition and re-build pictures that follow are printed with kind permission by our enlisted photographer, Bernard Wright. Anyone wishing to view more detailed views of this process can visit his website at: https://bernard-wright.smugmug.com/

The demolition and preparation process begins.

Our business went from strength to strength with a whole new audience base from far and wide. This was largely thanks to the membership scheme which made our customers feel a personal part of what we were achieving. The 'live' satellite events we now screened had become so popular and it became a pleasure to get to know these new patrons on first name terms. I always made a special effort to be attired in a proper evening dress so as to make their evening a little more special, and from the many comments received, it was well worth the effort, much to the bemusement of some of the younger members of the team. They just didn't understand the word etiquette anymore, which is sad really.

The same can be said for the film side of our business. The vast difference I had always emphasised between a conventional cinema in comparison to a modern-day multiplex had now been realised as our many patrons pointed out.

For me, now pretty much fully settled in again after my initial comeback, my role of 'Live Events Front of House Manager' had allowed me to bring the personal touch back to the patrons. I continued this approach with our cinema audiences too, as the film side of our business was going from strength to strength. They loved it and I thrived on it.

Welcome

The highlight of my new role was the time I arranged for a very special lady who had been housebound for a very long time to venture out and visit the cinema to see her favourite performer in a 'live' concert. Yes, of course it was Andre Rieu.

Mrs Daphne Catton, now in her 92nd year, has always held a special place in my heart as the very first person I interacted with on my first days in Bury St Edmunds. She was the kiosk attendant at the old Abbeygate and obviously noticed just how unsettled I felt being completely isolated from family and friends for the very first time in my life. From that very first evening, she took me under her wing so to speak and I always looked upon her as a surrogate mother from that moment on.

During all my years here, she has always been in the background, following with interest my every movement both at the cinema and in my family life. This was my way of saying, "Thank you, Daphne."

It turned out to be a very emotional meeting with the local Bury Free Press in attendance and they did us both proud. She still talks about that night to this day; yes indeed, it was a very special occasion.

Pat arranges cinema visit for his 'surrogate mum'

BY PAUL DERRICK

Renowned Abbeygate Cinema manager Pat Church arranged a special trip to the venue for his 93-year-old 'surrogate mum' who has been housebound for months.

Pat arranged for Daphne Catton to visit the cinema, in Hatter Street, Bury St Edmunds, on Sunday for a live screening of her favourite musician Andre Rieu's Maastricht Concert.

Daphne, who ventured out after being hospitalised and housebound for nine months, holds a 'special place' in Pat's heart with a bond formed when he began work as a projectionist at the cinema 52 years ago.

He said: "I came to Bury in 1966 as a shy lonely 19-year-old who had just left his family and friends behind.

"Daphne at that time was a kiosk attendant and I suppose in some ways she became my surrogate mother.

"She was always someone I could talk to and we clicked as you do with some people.

"For the last 52 years we've always been very close."

Pat organised the visit to 'get her out of the doldrums' and presented her with a bouquet of flowers before the screening.

The 72-year-old, who is semi retired and is the cinema's 'casual manager', said: "It was a dream come true for me.

"It was something I've always wanted to do for her and to be able to do it for this purpose made my day as much as her's, I was at the front (of the building) to greet her and it was quite an emotional moment for both of us.

"I've spoken to her and she can't get over it. It couldn't have gone better."

Pat Church presents a bouquet to Daphne Catton before the screening of Andre Rieu's Maastricht Concert

Whilst the new screens were being designed, the priority switched to an ambitious re-style of the front of the cinema This included creating a new foyer and box office space. Planning permission was the first obstacle encountered as we would be changing the original frontage to create a new and modern look, whilst still keeping a traditional appearance of this listed building. With the plans all approved, it was full steam ahead to create this much needed new space.

We opened up the shared foyer space of the old cinema/bingo entrances which also meant breaking through into the current entrance shared by No 4 and Abbeygate. This would create a complete walkthrough for restaurant and cinema patrons alike. However, nothing was straight forward and the front of the building was riddled with underground cellars and passages. These had to be strengthened before any re-build above them could take place.

I find it such a shame that these fascinating areas will never be viewed by members of the public, however I have ascertained permission to include a montage of Bernard Wrights more detailed views of these areas that were uncovered whilst the different walls and ceilings were being removed.

Once all of the shoring up work was behind us, it was full steam ahead to get on with the first stage that we so desperately needed, but another problem to overcome was the noise factor. The new foyer area being developed was situated directly beneath Screen 2. This meant a delicate juggling act had to take place as we were too busy to even think about closing the screen for an unlimited duration.

A plan was devised which saw to it that the builders had a screening schedule. This allowed them to accommodate the noisy jobs between performances. However, it worked better in theory than in practice as many of the sub-contractors that came to carry out specialist works were alien to this request, and normally they only had limited amounts of time to complete their tasks. Luckily for us, we had very understanding customers, most of whom were just as excited as us in seeing this work underway.

New foyer space and our New Look frontage

Once work was complete, we opened this area immediately, much to the delight of all our patrons. For the first time since the opening of the Central all those years ago, we now had room to accommodate our audiences.

Now, remember that 'big' shock I was telling you about?

Shortly after the opening of our new foyer, on 5 November 2019, we received an email from BAFTA (British Academy of Film, Television and Art). They host a 'For the Love of Film' competition annually. I had been nominated and was currently being considered by the selection board of that year's competition, for long standing work at the Abbeygate Cinema.

Later that same evening, as I was telling my colleagues at work all about this nomination, fireworks started going off overhead and it all seemed so surreal. After some investigation work, I tracked down those responsible for nominating me. However, they wished to remain anonymous and I respected their wishes.

My name had been selected from over 300 nominees and I was shortlisted in the final ten places. Two winners would be selected from a jury of five industry experts. These winners would then be invited to the 2020 EE/BAFTA awards ceremony at the Royal Albert Hall in London. The winning entrants would be announced in six to eight weeks' time, so there was not too much time to ponder on it.

I was so busy at site level that the weeks just rolled on by, but once the news hit the streets, the response and good luck messages became completely overwhelming (and it was only a nomination!).

The local press got in on the act but, for me regardless of the final outcome, the name Abbeygate Cinema was way up there as the No1 runner, extolling all the good works of past, present and future.

Unfortunately, I experienced that George Lazenby syndrome again as the notification of the final results arrived. All five jury members had commented about what a fantastic group of finalists they had had to choose from and that they had found it very difficult to make their decisions. I had not been selected as a winner this year, but I should consider entering again next year.

Admittedly, I was deeply disappointed and I felt I had let everybody down that had put my name forward, but looking back at the press reviews and to experience all of the numerous good wishes from the patrons and friends, I may not have won, but the name Abbeygate had firmly been placed with BAFTA.

Abbeygate's redevelopment programme by now was well underway despite several costly setbacks that had included the Asbestos removal and the strengthening of the underground vaults and cellars. Almost each time a wall was removed, another problem would emerge. By now, the project was into a six-figure sum and because we were a private, independent business, no funding or grants were forthcoming. Lyn Goleby never faltered though and the development continued.

During one of our regular manager meetings, I suggested that maybe we could involve the public to help fund our development. Our loyal customers had always been behind us, so perhaps we should now give them the opportunity to become involved with the redevelopment project and support the dream I had always had of this becoming a community-based cinema.

With the whole team in agreement, we launched our building block fundraising campaign. The idea behind this was to build on all the good wishes from our patrons who had watched and supported our steady growth over the past ten years. Their generous donation would be recognised in the form of an engraved wooden plaque which would be displayed prominently as part of the new décor. This would also ensure their support for a future film going generation.

The response to this idea, once put into practice, completely overwhelmed me, and in a short period of time, the project was well above anything I had ever anticipated.

Although the new foyer and entrance was in use, we wanted to create a setting to have an official opening. This came about with a very generous offer from Lionsgate Films who were releasing the film, *The Personal History of David Copperfield*. This film had aroused much appeal and interest as many location shots had taken place in and around Bury St Edmunds and Suffolk. In recognition of this, they honoured us with a special preview-showing with all proceeds being donated to our 2020 Building Blocks fundraising campaign. Plans were formulated by the entire Abbeygate team to incorporate this event into an official opening of the new foyer area. This would also include a Q&A session within the demolition area that would become our new screens, an area never before seen by the public. There would also be a short talk by our project manager, Chris which would serve as an introduction to the commencement of the film.

The evening was a complete success right from the word go! So many people wanted to brave the ice-cold elements in viewing this barn-of-a-place building site that was to become our premier screen along with a smaller select arts function screen. The questions seemed never-ending as small groups just seemed to follow each other. For me, as I was their host, I attempted to answer the many questions that were mostly based around the generics of the building. It's a wonder I didn't end up with hypothermia, but we soon warmed up when it was time to take our seats to watch *David Copperfield*.

Showing off our new foyer and facilities

Welcoming our guests to this very special evening

With the grand opening behind us, the builders set about developing our desperately needed new toilet block. Again, this was to be situated in a completely re-structured part of the original building, but once false walls and ceilings began to be removed, a lot of the original architecture was discovered which was in keeping with the historic ambiance we were trying to create. It seemed so wrong to wall it all back up again, so we experienced another delay whilst architects took time busily modifying their drawings for this area. Ironically, part of this new toilet area was where my old office had been, which, over 35 years, had experienced a considerable amount of 'bullshit' from people emphasising many point of views.

The demolition of my old office and stock room areas

It was always my intention to conclude this book with the opening of our two new screens, but of course the Corona virus pandemic has caused us to close, along with every other cinema and restaurant in the UK. I anticipate that it will be another year, at the very least, before we open up to a new era for this amazing cinema.

This means that my reminiscences have now caught up to where we are, as a site today.

The building work continues and, slowly, but surely, the new developments are taking place.

The old Periscope system in Screen 2 has been removed. A digital projector is being housed in the shaft where the mirrors were once situated, which will finally allow direct projection and a much-improved picture quality.

Moving forward, our plan is that once we are allowed to be up and running again, we will show off just what's in store for everyone and put to good use the already completed areas, as they become available, just as we did with the entrance and foyer.

We will then turn our attention to the premier screen. This project is such a mammoth undertaking and there is much work still to do. To open each individual area as and when is paramount to both us and our patrons! The partly completed premier screen is taking shape each day and now looking something like this.

It is still my intention to be there on the opening night, properly attired, to greet everyone into what should be a start to the next 100 years.

Epilogue (Part 1)
The Interviews

Over the many years I have had many interviews over all forms of media. I thought that it would be a fitting conclusion to this book to include a few press quotes, questions and answer sessions.

Bury Free Press

"We have had so many changes, it is like a new job every few years," he said. *"I started on February 16 1966 – it was a whole different world back then."*

"My whole aim has been to see our backstreet theatre become an important part of the community – that has been my dream."

From the digital revolution, heralding the end of 35mm, to the construction of Bury's multiplex Cineworld on Parkway – the cinema has never been allowed to stand still.

"You have to keep on changing," said Pat. *"Many people said to me when the Cineworld was built 'that will be the final nail in the coffin for Abbeygate,' but we are still here."*

"I think the opening of Cineworld was the making of us; we had to offer something different to survive, and now we are thriving."

The cinema and the personal, caring and intimate service Pat has pioneered, is more than just thriving – plans to 'finally' expand back into the third screen they vacated decades ago, are currently in the pipeline.

"40 years ago, they cut up the building and next door was turned into a bingo hall, and for 40 years I have been trying to reverse it," explained Pat.

"When the bingo hall closed [Winners Bingo in September 2014], the opportunity was there. It is not just about wanting to expand now, we need to, we have more people trying to visit us than we have room."

Pat has stared closure in face on several occasions. The first time was in 1975, when he asked for six months as manager to see if he could turn the business around – the rest is history.

When asked if he had an idea when he might retire, Pat laughed off the suggestion. "I have never thought about it," he said, "I want to see in the expansion first so I am not leaving yet."

The regular cinemagoers of Bury have become like a family to Pat, who admits he has to spend quite a bit of time just making sure he catches up with everyone before the films start.

"My life is the cinema," he said. Every big moment of my life has a movie title to go with it. I met my wife in 1966 when I was just a young lad – she and her mother moved into the flats that used to adjoin the cinema and her kitchen window looked out onto the projection room.

"The chief projectionist invited her to watch 'The Man From U.N.C.L.E' from the projection room and you could say it was love at first sight."

When Pat got engaged to Geraldine, who also works alongside him, he took her to see 'the Sound of Music'. "Our song is Edelweiss," he added.

This is a questionnaire I compiled for a local magazine.

I was five years old when I had my very first cinema experience. Over the next 68 years, films have been my staple diet. I have seen literally thousands of movies of all different genres, yet every event throughout my life is marked with a film title, and for that reason I could never choose a number one film. So here are five films that have had an everlasting memory for all different reasons:

The only exception to this would be any Marlon Brando film. Don't ask me why, but I could never take to this actor and dreaded being shut in a projection room all day with him staring back at me.

The Magnificent Seven

I always liked westerns from a very early age. They were, to me, always fantasy stories you could never relate to. This film had an all-star cast of my favourite heroes and it completely captivated me, and still does.

The Longest Day

As I was born just after the end of the Second World War, during my younger years, stories of that era were often a general topic. This film, in particular, brought many of those overheard stories back to reality.

Chitty Chitty Bang Bang

As a projectionist I loved showing musicals, watching the audience below you nodding away to the different songs or rocking with laughter at the fun parts. This film was a prime example and I would spend my days whistling or humming my favourite tunes.

Jaws

Now this was a film that completely fascinated me, as did most of the Stephen Spielberg productions. I suppose, in my mind, he took over from Alfred Hitchcock, another director I always followed.

The Green Book

This title brings me up to date and still holds my first spot for last year. I have seen it several times now and can't wait for my next viewing. It had all the right ingredients – comedy/drama/music/suspense.

1966

This has to be a milestone date in my life as this is when I decided to leave home and venture into this strange sounding town, Bury St Edmunds, where they all seemed to talk and sound different from those in Peterborough that I had left behind, but the Abbeygate Cinema beckons and here I come.

1970

The Abbeygate no more: as the business was sold off to a forward-thinking company who wanted to have two smaller cinemas and incorporate a bingo hall, hence the name change to Studios 1&2 and Social Bingo Club. This was also the first major change in projection methods, as film was now sent to the projector from a giant film carrier that would hold a full feature on one spool.

1975

This is the day I elected to take on the management role so as to stop the cinemas from being closed down. It turned out to be a very rocky ride as this company was having a very turbulent time, but I would not have changed my decision for the world.

1985

Suddenly, and without warning, the cinema was taken over by another company; little did we know just how many times this was to happen in future years, but each time we all as a team banded together and gave them our best shot. The highlight for me was the fun day as dressing up in a 'Fievel' costume for the Bury Carnival.

During the next 20 years, we had many such fun events, such as *The Lion King*. We actually had a lion cub in the cinema playfully tearing the posters up and anything else he could get his paws into, what a laugh.

Bury festival time, and we arranged an outdoor cinema experience in the Abbey Gardens. What a memorable day, and the sun shone on everyone. For the film, *Brassed Off,* we had the Stowmarket brass band playing in our foyer. Then for the 'Royal Wedding', for our early experimental attempt at 'live' satellite projection, we had an open house for anyone that wanted to pop in and view this event on the 'big' screen.

After being here for the past 54 years, my final achievement was to encourage our latest owners to reinstate the name 'Abbeygate Cinema'. What goes round comes round. So just watch this space, we ain't finished yet!

Epilogue (Part 2)
In Pictures

As mentioned earlier, here is a selection of photos, by Bernard Wright, of the redevelopment in its different stages:

Entrance to New Screens Area

Arch ceiling structure of old central   *Separation wall*

Stage Area That is Going to Become Screen Four

The underground section below the entrance and the new foyer where much work had to done to strengthen its structure before the above reconstruction could start.

The architectural features that were discovered when removing inner walls and ceilings and also the Georgian fireplace that was complete with gas pipes for lighting. Plans are in progress to repair and expose these for all to see once again.

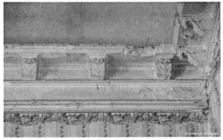

The re-routed fire escape takes you on a new journey, not seen before by the general public.

The amount of preparation work to open up the segregated foyer area and get the floor levels to match with the adjoining premises so as to become an open plan area was an unbelievable challenge, but the end result is amazing.

Epilogue (Part 3)
Gone, But Not Forgotten

In conclusion, I would consider it wrong not to include the three (long gone) small independent cinemas within the Suffolk area. Although I never had the fortune of working in any of them, I always had an affectionate feeling whilst following their fight for survival in the later days. I think that, most likely, they reminded me of my grass roots at the New England in Peterborough.

The Kingsway Cinema Newmarket

Located in Newmarket, Suffolk. The Kingsway Cinema was opened on 31 December 1926, very much like the old Central, it was a conversion of a mansion, known as Stamford House, which had been home to the Earls of Stamford & Warrington. The auditorium was built at the rear of the premises, just like the Central.

During its heyday, the Kingsway revelled in upgrading with all the new technology, as it became available. From its opening with its original sound on disc system, then in 1930 the new innovation that was to prove to be unbeatable for decades to come. It was, of course, film, with its own soundtrack.

In 1931, they installed the state-of-the-art British Talking Pictures (BTP) sound system. In 1955, they upgraded again when CinemaScope was installed and its big launch film was a screening of *Lucky Me* starring Doris Day.

The Kingsway Cinema was closed on 28 May 1977. It was then converted into the Coronet Social Club. And the rest, as they say, is history.

The Gainsborough Sudbury

I never went inside this cinema, as on the day that I made my one and only visit, it was closed; open evenings only! The reason I wanted to include it was the fact I seemed to know so much about its past history due to Hugh Berry starting his cinema career off at this site. Just like me, he wormed his way into the projection room and made his mark. We spent many hours talking about cinemas that we had previous association with, and once again the history side of each cinema completely fascinated me.

It opened in June 1912 and was named as The Gainsborough Theatre in affection of famous local artist, Thomas Gainsborough. The building kept that title until the early 1970s when taken on by a succession of independent operators who dropped the 'Theatre' title to become Gainsborough Cinema. This was done in the hope of generating new interest, but alas this was a dark era for so many small-town venues, and in 1982, it succumbed to the inevitable and closed its doors after its final screening of Dustin Hoffman in *Tootsie*.

The Palace Thetford

Geoff High pointing out the very last film he would be screening at the Palace

Of all the local independent cinemas, this was my favourite and I would often pop over on evenings when I wasn't working. These were days when I was still single and unattached. It was always a pleasure to see Geoff High, the manager/projectionist. Likewise, should he be in Bury for any reason, he would always visit our projection room.

Again, I was fascinated in hearing the history of the Palace which opened in 1913 and was operated by a former showman/fairground operator, Mr barker. He successfully nurtured the cinema which he had named 'The Peoples Palace' for the next 17 years. However, due to old age and it's need for upgrading, he sold it on to Mr Ben Culey Jr., who duly set about the promised upgrade and introduced the then modern projection techniques that included 'talkies'. He also renamed it to 'Palace Cinema', a name that would live out its lifetime over the next 35 years, surviving several dark periods.

When he went into partnership with Breckland Cinemas Ltd, they began to introduce bingo on a couple of nights each week to prop up the fall in cinema attendances. It struggled on until 1976, when Ben Culey bowed out and Breckland became the sole owners for the next few years.

However, they could not stem the downward spiral until Mr Keith Waterman took them on. He was the proprietor of Breckland Cinemas Ltd and was, by that time, well into the bingo game. The other cinema that was now under the Breckland banner was in Brandon and a full-time bingo hall, so in 1984 the Palace finally hit the dust after the last showing of Nicolas Cage in *Valley Girls*.

The building was now to become a bingo hall and renamed 'Winners Bingo' to make it uniform with its partner in Brandon. Deals were done for Breckland to also take over the bingo operation at the Hatter Street site in Bury St Edmunds.

As I previously said that cinema history fascinated me, and although they were individual businesses, there were so many similarities in their history. The people who operated them, from whatever part of the country they were situated in, were also of a similar nature; know what I mean?

Closing Comments…

It makes me wonder just what cinema history there will be for future generations. Can anyone really see a modern-day multiplex having such a chequered history. They all seem such faceless supermarket syndrome complexes.

Many people ask me, "Why do you still do it?"

I can't give a definitive answer. I can only say that I'm a great believer of 'fate'. My life always seemed to be mapped out for me. It's not until you look back over your life and see how all the pieces fitted together that you can start to understand this.

My parting words…

Although I have stepped back into a lesser capacity on the work front, I could never give in completely. To me it would be unthinkable. I would miss being even a small part of this business just too much.

I am so lucky to have the unreserved support of my family behind me, and I now focus all of my efforts to being present to open the new '4'-screen Abbeygate Cinema just as soon as the world gets back to normality. Here's to the future…

But, hang on a cotton-picking minute. The future has arrived. Would you believe that during the time it has taken to proofread and edit this book, the work on the preparation of the Premier Screen has raced away at breakneck speed, and I can proudly present it as a conclusion to my story.

My lifetime dream of seeing this building returned to one complete cinematic venue has been partly realised with the opening of the Premier Screen, well ahead of schedule.

It's onwards and upwards now as we focus on our specialist Arts Screen which will complete the transformation, but for now I couldn't be happier to be able to welcome you all to our new addition at the Abbeygate Cinema, and wish you all 'Happy Cinema Going' for the next millennium.

My ending phrase is a quote from my dear old Mum!

"Night Night Folks."

Appendix

In conclusion to putting my life in cinema into book form, it has never been a `one man band' I have always felt blessed to being surrounded by such a caring team and encouraging public, both past and present.

Even today I have this uncanny feeling of being watched over by the two most influential people in my life:

LEN my cinema mentor the man who took me under his wing at the tender age of twelve and started off the learning process.

DAD his interest and encouragement both in my work and family life, never faltered.

Even today I still feel their presence around me.

It just don't get no better than this, but a few weeks ago this envelope dropped onto the doormat with the words ON HER MAJESTY'S SERVICE emblazoned across it, for what seemed like an eternity I just stood staring at it completely dumbfounded.

Argh I thought they are looking for a new James Bond.

NO seriously it appears I have been awarded the British Empire Medal what an ending to this story. I excepted this on behalf of everyone out there that has supported the Abbeygate Cinema during my 55years in situ. You are the heroes. It's a community award: This has been recognized by Suffolk's Lord Lieutenant. Who has kindly agreed to hold the investiture at the Abbeygate Cinema later this year.

Cheers everyone!

Bury Free Press

ﾞILIFFE MEDIA

Friday, June 3, 2022 | www.buryfreepress.co.uk

Pat Church, of Abbeygate Cinema, has been awarded a BEM in the Queen's Birthday Honours.

More Honours news: Page 3

Pat honoured with BEM

Cinema's famous face is rewarded for services to the community

Paul Derrick
paul.derrick@iliffepublishing.co.uk

A cinema legend celebrating his own jubilee and an 80-year-old secretary in her seventh decade working at a US airbase are among those recognised in the Queen's Birthday Honours.

Pat Church, who is synonymous with the Abbeygate Cinema in Bury St Edmunds and this year marked his 60th in the industry, has been awarded a British Empire Medal (BEM) for services to the community.

He joined the picture house, in Hatter Street, aged 19 as a second projectionist - having started his career as a 12-year-old, working three evenings a week at a cinema in Peterborough before becoming full time aged 15 - and was instrumental in saving the venue from closure several times.

The 75-year-old said: "It's completely overwhelming - it still hasn't sunk in. I shall accept the honour on behalf of all the cinemagoers in Bury - without them I wouldn't be here."

In his nomination, Pat was hailed as an 'indomitable fighter' for persevering through numerous challenges and changes.

"The Abbeygate Cinema has been threatened with closure so many times," he said. "I'm on my 16th official ownership since I came to Bury. It did close once for three weeks until we could get new sponsors. It's always been a challenge."

During his career Pat, whose autobiography The Smallest Show on Earth was published in 2017, has arranged theatre, opera, ballet and orchestral experiences as well as dementia friendly screenings.

In lockdown, he set up a befriending telephone service 'Chat with Pat' for those isolated or alone and he rescued and restored a 100 year old wall mural at the cinema.

Now the venue's heritage and events manager, he has organised a series of 'talk and tours' about the history of the building and set up a memorabilia room full of fascinating items including messages from pupils at St Louis Catholic Middle School in 2008 when the venue, then named the Hollywood, had to shut. The tours are at 11.30am, 1.30pm and 3.30pm on June 7, 13, 14, 19 and 21.

He said: "I feel very lucky actually because I've been in a career and job which interests everyone for all different manner of reasons.

"Having been here so many years I know everyone personally - it's like your friends coming to see you."

1. Ensign Kazuo Sakamaki, the only Japanese to survive the midget submarine attack on Pearl Harbor, 7 December 1941. He was captured by American forces after swimming to a beach in Oahu the day after the raid, becoming the first Japanese serviceman taken prisoner by the United States in the Second World War.

2. Kazuo Sakamaki's midget submarine beached on Oahu Island in Hawaii, 8 December 1941.

3. A Japanese Type-A midget submarine being recovered from Pearl Harbor by the US Navy.

4. Sakamaki's midget submarine hastily secured to the beach by the US Army after beaching.

. A lifeboat from the Union Oil Company tanker *Montebello*, sunk by the Japanese submarine *I-21* off the coast of California on 23 December 1941. The Japanese skipper had attempted to machine-gun the survivors in the lifeboats, one of the earliest examples of Japanese naval war crimes. Eight Japanese submarines hunted off the United States west coast throughout December, sinking many American tankers and merchant ships close to the shore.

. A house wrecked by a Japanese shell in Sydney following a short bombardment by the Japanese submarine *I-24* on the night of 8/9 June 1942. Shortly afterwards another Japanese submarine, the *I-21*, surfaced in front of the town of Newcastle and unleashed a further bombardment using her deck gun.

7. Commander Harvey Newcomb RN, attached to the Royal Australian Navy and the officer in charge of anti-submarine defences in Sydney Harbour in 1942 when the Japanese launched their midget submarine attack. Newcomb had warned Rear Admiral Muirhead-Gould, the British naval officer in charge of the harbour, that the early warning submarine detection system known as the 'indicator loop system' was not being monitored correctly. His warning was proved tragically right when the Japanese raided Sydney Harbour on 31 May 1942 after successfully penetrating the harbour detection system.

8. Japanese midget submarine *A21* under the command of Sub-Lieutenant Keiu Matsuo penetrated Sydney Harbour of the night of 31 May 1942. Severely battered by attacks from Australian patrol boats, the damaged submarine was eventually sunk by depth charges. The *A21* was later discovered on the harbour floor, its engines still running. Pictured being recovered after the attack.

9. HMAS *Kattabul*, a converted ferry being used as a naval accommodation vessel in Sydney Harbour on 31 May 1942. Struck by a single Japanese torpedo fired from Lieutenant Ban's midget submarine *A*, twenty of the Australian and British sailors sleeping aboard her were killed.

10. Japanese midget submarine *A14*, which was part of the attack force launched against Sydney Harbour on the night of 31 May 1942. Crewed by Ensign Chuman and Petty officer Onori, the *A14* became entangled in anti-torpedo nets after partially penetrating the harbour. Chuman fired detonation charges that killed himself and Omori when Australian harbour patrol vessels came to investigate. The wrecked submarine was later recovered for technical study and public display.

11. Chief Warrant Officer (Flying) Nobuo Fujita. A former navy test pilot, he was the first man to bomb the continental United States by flying a small reconnaissance aircraft off the Japanese submarine *I-25* to attack the forests of Oregon on two occasions in September 1942. Fujita is pictured in flying kit shortly before his first mission to the American west coast.

12. The Port Orford Lighthouse in Oregon, which Nobuo Fujita used as a navigational beacon when he was catapulted from the deck of the Japanese submarine *I-25* in September 1942 to bomb America. The loneliness of this stretch of the US west coast was ideal for the submarine launched air raids the Japanese undertook, to drop incendiary bombs on the dense forests, inland from the coast, in an attempt to spark a major conflagration that would threaten American economic interests, tie down thousands of troops, and threaten local communities.

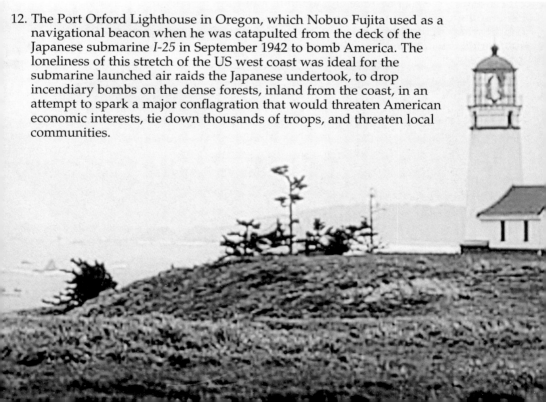

13. A Japanese Navy Kawanishi H8K1 four-engine naval flying boat which was nicknamed the 'Flying Porcupine' as it was armed with five 20mm cannon and four 7.7mm machine guns. Able to carry one ton of bombs, a pair of these huge aircraft conducted an elaborate second aerial attack of Pearl Harbor in March 1942.

14. Officers of the huge Japanese aircraft carrier submarine *I-400* pose in front of the waterproof hangar that contained three Aichi M6A1 Seiran torpedo bombers designed to launch devastating attacks on the Panama Canal and the American west coast. The end result of Japanese efforts to design and build technology capable of striking directly at the American home front, as Nobuo Fujita had first envisaged in 1942, each *I-400* class submarine was over 400 feet long, and was not surpassed in scale until the nuclear submarines of the 1960s. The class could cruise 35,000 miles without refuelling enabling the Japanese Navy to strike virtually anywhere in the world. Fortunately, the Japanese surrender came before these boats and their modern bomber aircraft could be used against the Allies.

15. The waterproof hanger aboard the *1-400* submarine. With their wings folded up and floats removed, three Aichi Seiran torpedo bombers were stowed inside. A separate magazine below the hanger held aerial torpedoes and bombs for the aircraft. The aircraft were launched by means of catapult built into the submarine's deck forward of the hanger. On returning to the submarine, the aircraft would land in the sea and then be winched aboard by a huge crane.

16. Japanese Navy Aichi M6A1 Seiran 'Storm from the Sky' torpedo bomber. Capable of nearly 300 miles per hour, and able to carry a maximum bomb load of just over 1,200 pounds, the Seiran had a range of over 650 miles. The *I-400* class aircraft carrier submarines could wait far off the enemy coast and launch the Seiran bombers on surprise attacks on enemy shipping, harbour facilities or cities.

attention needed to be paid to every contact recorded. The Japanese midget submarine attack on Pearl Harbor in 1941 had, if anything, driven this point home to Newcomb. The system, however, was not functioning correctly and crucially the first loops would fail to alert the Australians to a submarine penetration of the harbour. On the evening of 31 May 1942 the three Japanese midget submarines approaching Sydney Harbour were not detected by the first stages of the indicator loop system, because parts of the system were out of action. Midget *A14* passed over several more indicator loop cables as she made for the west-gate boom and net opening. At the naval recording station at South Head a contact was noted several times, but was dismissed as probably one of several ferries and patrol boats moving about the harbour. This point highlights Newcomb's very real concerns over correct monitoring and recording by local naval personnel. Part of the problem was the fact that the system was unable to differentiate between different types of vessels, so it was down to the operator and his superiors to determine a likely cause of the contact.

The first actual confirmed detection of a midget submarine inside the harbour, and inside the defences, was by pure chance. The Australian Maritime Services maintained waterborne lookouts around the harbour entrance, entrusted to watch the gap and to make sure no one interfered with any of the equipment. Watchmen James Cargill and William Nangle were sitting in a punt when they noticed something unusual between the anti-torpedo nets and the west channel light. Cargill said in a report to Muirhead-Gould, now promoted to the rank of rear-admiral, that, 'We thought at first it was a fishing launch with no lights and, knowing that that was not allowed, I went in the rowing boat to investigate.' Cargill rowed up alongside the unidentified craft and 'found it was a steel construction about 4 or 5 feet above the water, which looked like two large cylinders with iron guards around them.'[6] Cargill immediately rowed over to the patrol boat HMAS *Yarroma*, which was about eighty yards away, and reported what he had seen to the officer commanding. When asked by the officer what he though it was, Cargill replied, 'I thought it was a submarine or a mine'. Because the naval officer refused to take the *Yarroma* closer to the object, presumably fearing a magnetic mine, Cargill rowed a naval rating back over to the craft. By now the midget submarine's hull was partially visible, and the rating had no trouble in immediately identifying what it was.

Lieutenant Chuman onboard the *A14* by now realized that his craft was trapped in the Australian nets. Two hours after Cargill had first sighted and reported an object in the nets, at 10.30 p.m., the *Yarroma* sent the following signal to naval headquarters in Sydney: 'Object is submarine. Request permission to open fire.'[7] Another patrol boat, HMAS *Lolita*, came up and dropped several depth charges close to the midget that was followed by an infinitely bigger and louder detonation that woke up the entire harbour area. A booming echo ran the length of the harbour, bringing citizens to their windows and out onto the streets where all they could see were several searchlights scanning the waters. Lieutenant Chuman and Petty Officer Omori, realizing that they were trapped in the nets, and determined to avoid the disgrace of capture, had set the submarine's demolition charge, determined to kill themselves rather than face an ignominious confinement. Death had come instantly as the midget had blown itself to pieces. Admiral Muirhead-Gould looked now to the various ships' captains to begin moving their vessels around the harbour as an immediate anti-submarine strategy. The heavy cruiser USS *Chicago*, misidentified by Japanese aerial reconnaissance as the British battleship HMS *Warspite*, and the destroyer USS *Perkins* began, after a signal at 10.43 p.m., to take anti-submarine precautions.[8]

Sub-Lieutenant Ban in Midget *A* had decided upon a clever strategy for entering the harbour unchallenged, in a similar fashion to Sub-Lieutenant Yokoyama on the morning of 7 December 1941 who had placed his midget in the wake of the repair ship USS *Antares* and trailed her towards the open gate in the anti-submarine net protecting the entrance to Pearl Harbor. Although Ban's Midget *A* showed up on the indicator loop system at 9.48 p.m., Ban manoeuvred his submarine behind the Manly ferry that was just coming into the harbour.[9] His target was the USS *Chicago*, although Ban thought the vessel was the British battleship *Warspite*. Australian Naval headquarters, following the

116

two indicator loop crossings over cable no. 3, had finally begun to take some action. Two corvettes, HMAS *Geelong* and *Whyalla* each received signals to move out and investigate. In the meantime, Midget *A21* under Lieutenant Matsuo waited at the Harbour Heads while Ban launched his attack.

Neither of the Australian warships detailed to investigate the suspicious indicator loop reports was actually ready for combat. For a start, a majority of the crews from both of the vessels were ashore, on leave. The *Whyalla* was missing her captain who was on his farm three hours away by car, and the remaining crew was unfamiliar with new 20mm Oerlikon cannon fitted to the vessel. The *Geelong* could only run on one engine, the other one being under repair, and she had only one officer and five ratings aboard. Lieutenant Harry Tyrrell of the Royal Australian Naval Reserve ordered a Vickers machine gun located aft, manned and loaded. Incredibly, Tyrrell spotted Midget *A*'s conning tower cutting through the water heading towards Farm Cove, where the heavy cruiser HMAS *Canberra* was berthed. Tyrrell took an Aldis lamp and trained it on the midget's conning tower, ordering the Vickers gunner to open fire. The rating held his fire, however, as he believed that a nearby civilian ferry was too close to his line of fire.[10]   The USS *Chicago* was moored close to the *Canberra*. Lookouts aboard the American ship also spotted the midget's conning tower and turned on their searchlights to assist the gunners who began working the ships secondary armament. The *Geelong* finally joined in with bursts of Vickers fire, but the midget did not deviate too far from her course, moving towards the Sydney Harbour Bridge. The dockyard motorboat *Nestor* narrowly avoided colliding with the submarine. Midget *A* began to submerge as the water was churned by a hail of exploding shells and machine-gun bullets from vessels in the vicinity as they attempted to stop the little submarine from acquiring a target.

Midget *A21* under Lieutenant Matsuo entered the harbour unnoticed as all attention, and the shooting, was focused on Ban's Midget *A* deep inside the harbour proper. At 10.54 p.m. HMAS *Lauriana*, an unarmed patrol boat managed to illuminate with her searchlight the unmistakable shape of a small submarine's conning tower cutting through the still water. Immediately, as the brilliant white beam of the searchlight flashed through Matsuo's periscope, he ordered Tsuzuku to dive the boat. Although the *Lauriana* was powerless to attack the Japanese submarine she was able to call up some reinforcements on her radio, and alerted the armed patrol boat HMAS *Yandra*.[11] The *Yandra* closed up behind the *A21* as the midget proceeded down the east channel, the former taking six minutes to entirely close the gap between herself and the submarine until the midget disappeared beneath the forecastle. A hard impact was felt throughout the *Yandra*, confirming that she had successfully rammed the submarine. Lookouts reported that the submarine appeared to be submerging once the *Yandra* had sailed on about 100 yards after passing over the submarine's conning tower. Midget *A21* popped back to the surface about 600 yards from the *Yandra*, but by the time the gun crew had organized themselves it was found to be impossible to depress the gun sufficiently to hit the submarine. The *A21* submerged again, followed by six depth charges that rolled off the stern of the *Yandra*. The underwater detonations of the depth charges, each barrel's fuse having been set at 100 feet, caused more damage to the Australian vessels than the Japanese midget, which had dived to the bottom of the harbour and was now waiting for the anti-submarine attack to come to an end. On board the *Yandra* the explosions had caused the steering gear, anti-submarine gear, degaussing gear and telephone communication to aft to all fail. HMAS *Lauriana* had been lifted clear of the water by the explosions, also causing the vessel some minor damage.

Admiral Muirhead-Gould now issued two orders. Firstly, he ordered that all ferry operations in the harbour should continue, hoping that the assorted vessels movements might assist navy efforts in preventing the midget submarines from finding targets. Busy surface traffic would hopefully keep the midgets submerged, and therefore blind. Secondly, Muirhead-Gould ordered the dockyard and graving dock lights immediately extinguished on the Garden Island naval base, which was lit up like the proverbial Christmas tree, providing the enemy with light to find targets with their periscopes and a useful navigation point.

At 11.25 p.m. the dockyard was plunged suddenly into darkness. At 12.30 a.m. on the morning of 1 June Ban's midget surfaced close to Bradley's Head off Garden Island. Ban lined up his vessel as best he could on the now darkened anchorage and ordered Petty Officer Ashibe to fire both torpedoes. The first torpedo ran past the USS *Chicago*, missing the heavy cruiser and Ban's primary target by about 300 yards. It then passed beneath the Royal Netherlands Navy submarine *K-9* and continued on, eventually ploughing into the harbour wall directly beneath HMAS *Kuttabul*.[12] The *Kuttabul* was a former ferry being used as a navy accommodation ship, and the detonation of the Japanese torpedo beneath her was catastrophic. The vessel was lifted from the water, almost breaking in two as an enormous fountain of spray and debris plumed into the air over the stricken ship. The detonation smashed windows in surrounding houses, knocked out the lights at naval headquarters, and shook buildings to their foundations. Most of the sailors aboard the *Kuttabul* were in hammocks, which proved to be almost impossible to get out of as the ship twisted into the air and then sank rapidly into the harbour. Nineteen sailors were killed by the torpedo or drowned in their hammocks, and another seaman died later in hospital. Many others were injured or left in a state of shock from their ordeal. The Dutch submarine *K-9* was also badly damaged in the attack, though none of her crew received injuries. Ban's second torpedo tore past the USS *Perkins*, just missed the *Chicago* and then ran onto the foreshore but did not explode.[13] Lieutenant Tyrrell from HMAS *Geelong* was ashore when the *Kuttabul* was sunk and saw the beached Japanese torpedo as he rushed back to his vessel with new orders, the torpedo's propellers still running at full speed on the small beach, with a fluid leaking ominously out of the casing.

Many civilians believed that a Japanese invasion of Sydney was underway, the explosion of Ban's torpedo being so tremendous, and coming after the equally impressive self-destruction of Chuman's *A14* on the nets. The harbour was also ablaze with machine- gun and tracer fire and numerous detonations as Allied naval vessels, from heavy cruisers to small patrol boats, shot up anything resembling a midget submarine. As the morning progressed the navy started to recover from the initial shock of being under attack, and to organize a hunt for the two remaining Japanese midget submarines that were lurking in the harbour somewhere. It would be a hunt to their destruction. HMAS

Whyalla was ordered to leave Sydney Harbour and seek out the larger Japanese 'mother' submarines that were assumed to be close by awaiting the return of the midgets. An aerial search was also mounted in the hope of locating these submarines and destroying them. Just after 2 a.m. the *Chicago* and *Perkins* moved out to sea.[14] Less than an hour later as the *Chicago* was passing the northern tip of South Head a submarine periscope was spotted almost alongside the heavy cruiser. The warship's guns would not depress sufficiently to engage the submarine, but the sighting was reported to Admiral Muirhead-Gould. This midget was the *A21* under Lieutenant Matsuo that had survived the ramming and depth charge attacks of the *Yandra* four hours earlier. Due to mechanical failure, neither of the midget's torpedoes could be fired, so it is surmised that Matsuo attempted to use the *A21* as one giant torpedo, and ram his boat into the *Chicago* in the hope of detonating the torpedoes and killing himself and his crewman in true kamikaze style.

For several hours Australian patrol vessels reported contacts with submarines everywhere, and depth charges were dropped all over the harbour. Midget *A21* was eventually sunk by depth charges at 5 a.m. in Taylor Bay by HMAS *Yarroma*, assisted by HMAS *Steady Hour* and *Sea Mist*.[15] The midget submarine was later discovered on the harbour floor with its engines still running. Matsuo and Tsuzuku had both shot themselves. Sub-Lieutenant Ban and Midget *A* were never seen again, and the wreck of the boat has still not been discovered. It is suspected that Ban managed to get clear of the harbour and headed out into the open sea. Perhaps aware that attempting to reach any of the 'mother' submarines could have drawn Australian anti-submarine forces down on them it has been surmised than Ban scuttled his boat, killing himself and Petty Officer Ashibe. The bodies of Lieutenants Chuman and Matsuo, and Petty Officers Omori and Tsuzuku, were recovered from Midgets *A14* and *A21* respectively. Their bodies were taken ashore to a civilian funeral director's and prepared for cremation. On 9 June cremation of the Japanese sailors was duly conducted at the Eastern Suburbs Crematorium with full military honours. Chief among the dignitaries who attended the funeral service was Rear-Admiral Muirhead-Gould, who was to come under great criticism from the Australian public for granting the enemy such an honour while largely ignoring the deaths of twenty Australian and British sailors from HMAS *Kuttabul*. In response, Muirhead-Gould replied, '…should we not accord full honours to such brave men as these? It must take courage of the very highest order to go out in a thing like that steel coffin [a reference to the Type-A Midget Submarine]'.[16] However, the entire affair was to leave a bad taste in the Australian public's mouth, compounded by the fact that Muirhead-Gould was not even an Australian. In Japan the six dead submariners were immediately elevated to the status of war gods, and the ashes of the cremated men were returned to Tokyo by Australia.

The remains of the two midget submarines raised from the harbour bed, *A14* which was wrecked by the demolition charge, and *A21*, which had suffered some damage during depth charging, would go on to serve as a useful propaganda tool for Australia. From the two damaged midgets one complete example was reconstructed and toured rural New South Wales, Victoria and South Australia raising funds for the war effort. Eventually the composite submarine was delivered to the Australian War Memorial in Canberra in 1943, where it remains on display today. Incredibly, after all the efforts of both service personnel and civilians in foiling the Japanese attack on Sydney Harbour, not a single bravery or meritorious service award was made to any of the participants, even though many recommendations were submitted. Muirhead-Gould even went so far as to criticize Watchman James Cargill who had first spotted Midget *A14* caught in the anti-torpedo net, commenting that he was too slow in alerting the authorities to his discovery. In the end it was only the two watchmen, Cargill and William Nangle, who received an award, both men receiving paltry sums of money.

As the citizens of Sydney digested the impact of the midget submarine attacks in the days following the raid ,tensions remained high. Although the Royal Australian Navy and city authorities could correctly claim that the Japanese raid had been a failure, resulting in the known destruction of two of the raiders' crafts, people nonetheless realized that Sydney had had a close brush with disaster.

Commander Newcomb's January warning to Muirhead-Gould

regarding the correct monitoring of the indicator loops had proved prophetic, as all of the midget submarines had passed unnoticed over Sydney's early warning system until well inside the harbour. The Japanese had also been able to conduct an unchallenged aerial reconnaissance mission over the harbour before the attack in a Yokosuka E14Y1 floatplane piloted by Chief Warrant Officer Fujita from the submarine *I-25*, and it was really only pure luck that had prevented a significant warship such as the USS *Chicago* from being torpedoed. The death of twenty sailors aboard HMAS *Kuttabul* was serious enough, especially as it occurred deep inside a well-defended friendly harbour, and the death toll among Allied sailors would undoubtedly been more severe had not Lieutenant Matsuo's torpedo tubes malfunctioned. Sydney Harbour, even with an electronic early warning system in place and mostly functioning, had been penetrated with relative ease by three Japanese midget submarines that were crewed by suicidally determined and brave young submariners, none of whom returned from their mission.

Another factor that emerged soon after the attack were details of a virtually identical operation conducted by the Japanese just seventeen hours before Sydney Harbour was penetrated. Two midget submarines had successfully entered the Royal Navy's Indian Ocean base at Diego Suarez in Madagascar to wreak havoc, drawn from Rear-Admiral Noboru Ishizaki's Western Advance Flotilla, sailing out of Penang in Japanese-occupied Malaya into the Indian Ocean.

Madagascar had been invaded and occupied by the British between May 1942 and the eventual Vichy French capitulation in November, in an effort to deny the Japanese port facilities for their submarines in the western Indian Ocean. The initial phase of the occupation of northern Madagascar had been completed when the French had surrendered on 7 May after three days of resistance. The operation had cost the British 105 killed and 283 wounded, with Vichy French casualties amounting to approximately 150 killed and 500 wounded. All Vichy French resistance on Madagascar ended with a complete surrender on 6 November 1942. Had the Japanese managed to persuade the Vichy authorities to allow them to have based submarines in Madagascar, as they had persuaded the collaborationist government to allow

Japanese troops and aircraft into French Indochina just prior to Pearl Harbor, such a move would have placed the Japanese in an ideal position, sitting along Britain's Middle East and South African convoy routes. The British had successfully conquered northern Madagascar, and crushed Vichy French resistance in the region by May 1942, enabling the utilization of the port of Diego Suarez as an Allied naval base. The Japanese, however, were determined to attack the anchorage and hopefully destroy several of the warships moored within, in a surprise attack employing the Type-A Midget submarine and long range I-class boats. In Diego Suarez harbour on 30 May there was a collection of Allied warships and supply vessels riding at anchor. HMS *Karanja, Genista, Thyme, Duncan* and *Active*, all convoy escorts, were berthed alongside a hospital ship, the *Atlantis*, the merchantman *Llandaff Castle*, and an ammunition ship. A bigger fish for the Japanese to attempt to fry was the battleship HMS *Ramillies*.

On the evening of 30 May 1942, the Japanese fleet submarines *I-16* and *I-20* had each launched a midget several miles off the Madagascar anchorage, a third midget launch being cancelled aboard the *I-18* owing to mechanical problems. The two midgets, crewed by Ensign Katsusuke Iwase and Petty Officer Takazo Takata, and Lieutenant Saburo Akieda and Petty Officer Masami Takemoto respectively, would attempt to penetrate the port of Diego Suarez undetected and search out targets among a large number of British warships and merchant vessels moored inside. Iwase and Takata clambered into the confines of the Type A's cockpit, both armed with pistols. Iwase also symbolically carried a short tachi sword, denoting his officer rank and status, and highlighting the Japanese military's adherence to the samurai's Bushido code, 'which upheld the virtues of man-to-man combat in a machine age, and demanded that the Japanese soldier die rather than surrender'.[17]

As they approached the shallow harbour the Japanese crewmen dived their submarines to hopefully avoid Allied watchmen, and penetrated the port undetected. Darkness had fallen, but the light of a full moon bathed the busy anchorage and array of ships. Crewmen on the decks of the huge *Ramillies*, and aboard the nearby tanker *British Loyalty*, reported that they saw two conning towers negotiating the harbour entrance, though

123

strangely no immediate action was taken. At 8.25 p.m. Akieda began his torpedo attack. Lining up on the *Ramillies*, Akieda launched a single torpedo at the battleship. A few seconds later there was an enormous explosion that lit up the harbour, a massive plume of flame, debris and black smoke climbing into the humid night air, as the *Ramillies* reeled from the torpedo strike. A thirty-foot hole had been blown in the port side of the ship, water flooding into the steaming gash in her side. Men had been thrown down by the force of the explosion, or battered mercilessly against metal surfaces inside the ship, injuring themselves. Although the ship's damage control parties managed to save her from settling onto the muddy bottom of the harbour, intermittent power and communication failures throughout the rest of the night made their jobs very difficult. Fortunately for the British, Akieda must have assumed that he had crippled the battleship with a single strike, because he did not immediately launch his remaining torpedo at her. Close by, the captain of the *British Loyalty* ordered the crew to swing out the boats, and to raise the anchor. He rang the engine room telegraph to order the engineers to 'standby', but it was to take the tanker almost an hour to begin to move away from her berth. In the meantime Royal Navy corvettes, fast anti-submarine vessels, raced around the port, depth charging any suspicious targets in the hope of preventing further attacks. A signalman aboard the damaged *Ramillies* was searching the water for signs of the invisible attacker, when he saw the unmistakable wake of a torpedo running fast in the bright moonlight, heading not for the warship, but travelling to intercept the *British Loyalty*. The tanker was reversing noisily in its manoeuvres from its berth, directly into the path of the oncoming Japanese torpedo that was obviously intended to finish off the stricken *Ramillies*. Another booming explosion rolled out over the harbour as hundreds of pounds of high explosives detonated inside the tanker's engine room. The *British Loyalty* began to sink rapidly by the stern, and Captain Wastell ordered his crew to abandon ship. Officers worked frantically to fill the boats with the mainly Indian crewmen, launch them down the straining davits, and get the crew to safety aboard other ships in the harbour. Five crewmen were killed aboard the *British Loyalty*, but the loss of the tanker undoubtedly saved the battleship.

Akieda now attempted to leave the harbour and rendezvous with the *I-20* for recovery, but his midget ran aground and he was forced, along with his navigator, to abandon the vessel and swim to shore. The Japanese sailors were determined that they would not allow themselves to be captured by the British, and the two men set off on a long march across northern Madagascar hoping to be able to signal the *I-20* from shore and be rescued. Cornered by British soldiers on 2 June after fifty-nine hours on the loose, Akieda and Petty Officer Takemoto determined to go down fighting. Armed with two pistols and Akieda's short sword, the Japanese submariners managed to kill one British soldier and wound four others before they themselves perished in the firefight. The fate of Ensign Iwase and his midget remains a mystery to the present day, though it is surmised that he was probably sunk by mechanical failure or destroyed by British depth charging.

The British immediately suppressed details of the Diego Suarez attack, and, incredibly, they issued no warnings to other British and Commonwealth naval bases concerning the possibility of similar attacks being attempted by the Japanese. Sydney could, and more importantly, should, have been informed at some point during the intervening seventeen hours between the Diego Suarez raid and the discovery of Lieutenant Chuman's Midget *A14* stuck fast in the anti-torpedo nets in Sydney Harbour. Rear-Admiral Muirhead-Gould and the harbour's anti-submarine officer, Acting Commander Newcomb, were deliberately kept in the dark concerning the attack in Madagascar, even though both were Royal Navy officers seconded to assist the Australians. Such a warning of even a few hours would have been sufficient time for Muirhead-Gould to have placed Sydney Harbour on high alert, ordered the recall of patrol boat crews from shore leave, and taken blackout precautions to deny the enemy navigation points and light by which to locate target ships. He would also have been able to instruct Newcomb to make sure all indicator loop contacts were investigated, and not ignored as was the case on the evening of 31 May, and perhaps the Royal Australian Air Force could have begun patrols of the harbour approaches, as well as sweeps out to sea in case any larger Japanese submarines turned up. In any case, all this is conjecture, and, as it stood, the

Admiralty and British Government's secrecy meant that Muirhead-Gould and his staff were not alerted to increase their vigilance in the light of a realistic chance of attack.

Off Sydney, the five Japanese I-class submarines that had participated in the attack, three of which had actually launched midgets, remained on station for several days hoping that at least one of the midgets would attempt a rendezvous. Their captains eventually realized that all three submarines had been lost, and the five larger boats moved off to begin a successful campaign of interdicting merchant shipping along the Australian coast.

The Japanese 'mother' and support submarines that had launched the Second Special Attack Flotilla of Type-A midgets against Sydney Harbour on 30 May had spent several fruitless days and nights waiting for the return of some or all of the small vessels. None returned, which hardly came as a surprise to the Japanese following the fates of the midgets launched against Pearl Harbor six months previously, and the two dispatched to Diego Suarez less than a day before the Sydney operation. The young officers and men who had cast off from the big I-class submarines and penetrated Sydney Harbour had demonstrated in their letters and final words a willingness to die for the Emperor and their families, and a realization that they were probably on one-way missions for Japan. The five I-class submarines abandoned their vigil in early June and moved off up the Australian coast to in order to hunt merchantmen assigned as the second part of their mission into Australian waters.

Following the surprise midget submarine attack on Sydney, and several Japanese submarine attacks on merchant ships off the Australian coast, Sydney and the nearby port of Newcastle were closed to outward ship traffic. Convoys were immediately instituted for coastal commerce in a belated attempt to warn off Japanese submarines from further mercantile interdiction, leaving only the smallest coastal craft to fend for themselves. The RAAF, assisted by a squadron from the Netherlands East Indies Army Air Corps, conducted anti-submarine sweeps over the sea approaches to both ports and convoy routes along the coast, assisted by naval ships. All these late precautions, however, did not prevent a pair of Japanese submarines from the original

Sydney attack force from striking the Australian mainland in another daring and bold pair of attacks.

At dusk on 3 June, the Type-C1 submarine *I-24* was recharging her batteries while sitting on the surface, east of Sydney. Sharp-eyed lookouts spotted a coastal steamer making her way quietly along, quite alone, and Commander Hanabusa brought his boat to immediate readiness for attack. The ship was the 4,734-ton *Age* and Hanabusa fired a single torpedo at the ship but missed. The deck-gun was swung into action against the freighter, which was naturally attempting to make off as fast as possible, and four shells slammed out across the ocean as the merchant ship's radio operator called desperately for assistance. None of the shells found their marks, and the *Age* disappeared into the evening gloom.[18] When Hanabusa saw the ship disappear he assumed that he had managed to sink her, and recorded a victory for the *I-24* in his report of the action. About an hour and a half later Hanabusa had something genuine to report. Still east of Sydney, the *I-24* encountered the *Iron Chieftain*, a British coke carrier on her way from Newcastle to Whyalla. Hanabusa launched two torpedoes at the 4,800-ton ship, one of which struck the freighter squarely amidships on her portside, and within only five minutes the *Iron Chieftain* was gone, another victim of the Japanese inshore submarine campaign against Australia. Two days later a third target presented itself to the *I-24*, the 3,362-ton Australian merchantman *Echunga* when the Japanese submarine was about seventeen miles off Wollongong. On this occasion Hanabusa failed to achieve a hit on the freighter and broke off his attack.[19]

The Type-B1 *I-27* intercepted the Australian freighter *Barwon* (4,239-tons) off Gabo Island, New South Wales, on 4 June and attempted to sink her with both torpedo and gunfire. The *Barwon* managed to flee without sustaining any damage. Later that same day, the *I-27* was cruising through the Bass Strait, off Cape Howe, when she discovered two Australian iron ore carriers travelling in company. A Japanese torpedo struck the 3,353-ton *Iron Crown*, which sank quickly. The other vessel that was sailing with the doomed ship, the *Iron King*, opened fire on the surfaced Japanese submarine, but the *I-27* easily evaded the shots and made off.[20]

On the night of 8 June the *I-24* was laying about nine miles off the Macquarie Light, Sydney, preparing to move towards the city. Motoring on the surface, proceeding north-west towards the coast, Hanabusa quietly brought his boat close in to the Heads, the landmasses marking the entrance to Sydney Harbour. Hanabusa's plan was simple: unleash the deck-gun in the general direction of the famous Harbour Bridge. The silence of the night was suddenly shattered by the booming report of the submarine's deck-gun, followed by the whine of high-velocity shells that ploughed into the districts of Rose Bay, Woollahra, Bondi and Bellevue Hill. The Japanese gunners quickly loosed off ten shells then the *I-24* ceased firing and slinked away before the Australians had any time to respond to the surprise assault.

By sheer good luck no Sydneysiders were killed by the 140mm shells that came hurtling into the centre of their city in the dead of night, but some damage to property was caused. The *Sydney Morning Herald* reported that initially Sydneysiders thought they were being bombed instead of shelled: 'In the seaside suburbs many people mistook the scream of the shells for screaming bombs coming from aeroplanes. No planes, however, were reported over Sydney, and the [air raid] alarm was sounded merely as a precaution.'[21] Rather than taking shelter many local residents opted for a spot of sightseeing: '...people made for the open streets and stood in eager groups...watching the flashes [of the Japanese deck-gun]. There was no panic, though many listened intently, fearing that the explosions were caused by bombs and that they would hear the drone of planes overhead.'[22] When the air raid sirens began to wail, '...the lights of Sydney flickered out in a few seconds. Up to this stage, thousands of people all over the city had been merely passive watchers of the gun flashes, which had lit up the sky far to the west of the coastal zone.'[23]

With the sudden blackout, most residents hurried back to their homes, 'groping for matches and screened torches to enable them to get to their shelters'.[24] Why only a few of the ten shells fired by the Japanese actually detonated will probably never be known, but the poor performance of the munitions probably saved many lives throughout the city. The Japanese later contended that it was

128

because the shells were stored on the submarines' weather decks in the ready-use ammunition lockers close to the deck-gun that explained the high proportion of 'duds'. Moisture probably had penetrated the shells, making some malfunction occur.

The Australians (and the Americans who were also subjected to coastal deck-gun bombardments along the west coast) claimed that the Japanese were using the wrong type of projectile against shore targets. The Japanese armour-piercing shell was designed to penetrate the steel hull of a ship and explode within, and the tough shells simply passed straight through the softer brick walls of houses and business premises throughout Sydney, often failing to detonate but still causing considerable damage.

Be that as it may, Sydneysiders were awakened by the crash and thud of Japanese shells falling on four city districts. Of the ten shells fired by the *I-24*, nine buildings suffered resultant damage. The people of Sydney, however, were undaunted by their most recent brush with the enemy. 'In one case, when a woman discovered her kitchen had been destroyed by a direct hit, she calmly turned off the mains gas and steadfastly refused to leave her house.'[25] Ironically, the only resident who was injured in the attack was a German Jewish refugee who had fled from the Nazis. A Japanese shell ploughed into his apartment on Manion Avenue in Rose Bay, but failed to detonate. He was injured when '...a heavy metal lampstand fell on his leg when the shell hit the apartment, passed through the room in which his mother was sleeping and out onto a staircase. He was buried under the rubble.'[26] The *Sydney Morning Herald* reporter quickly on the scene gave this description of the action:

It [the Japanese shell] tore through the two brick thicknesses above the head of Mrs. Hirsch's bed, skidded along the wall flanking her bed, bursting the bricks through in a large gash, but not penetrating to the next room, then pierced the third wall of Mrs. Hirsch's room below the end of her bed, tore through the two walls flanking a hall, and finished up on a staircase between the first and second floors. Mrs. Hirsch was showered with bricks. Her bed was broken by the falling debris. She herself escaped unscathed.[27]

The shell, which was still live, 'lay on the staircase for a time, then an air-raid warden carried it into a nearby street. A little later it was removed to Woollahra Park oval and buried.'[28] The offending shell was eventually defused by the navy and found a new purpose in propping open the doors to the Woollahra Council Chambers until recently moved to a museum. Other residents in the apartment block also had lucky escapes. The wife of resident air-raid warden W.R. Clarkson recalled later that day:

I was awakened by the first shot, and looked out the first floor window and found that the rest of the occupants of the flat building were awake. I was looking out the window when I heard a loud swish and a bang. Pieces of brick from the wall hit me. I then took my two children to a room we had specially prepared for air raids.[29]

In another flat inside the block ten-year old Barbara Woodward, whose father was another air-raid warden, recalled:

Mummy fell down, and I was frightened. I heard a bang in the roof and grabbed my kitten, 'Mr. Churchill,' and went with the other children to a room at the back of the flat. 'Mr. Churchill' was not frightened.[30]

Outside another apartment block a Japanese shell exploded in Plumer Street, Rose Bay, the blast:

...shattered portions of the walls and all the windows and glass doors of Yallambee Flats. People in several flats had narrow escapes from injury as debris fell around them. A woman sleeping in a enclosed verandah was slightly injured by flying glass.[31]

The noise of the Japanese gunfire had drawn many of the apartment block's residents to their windows before the shell landed. One resident recalled later that day:

We all seemed to be waiting for something to happen...Then we got it. There was a terrific blast, and the whole building trembled. Everyone rushed to air-raid shelters, but there was no panic.[32]

Wardens and police herded thousands of local residents into air raid shelters across the city. Patients at local hospitals were carried down to basement areas for their protection, though local civil defence authorities did some grumbling after the raid concerning some Sydneysiders who had refused to cooperate with them when ordered to evacuate their houses or to take shelter. The evacuations took far longer than the short Japanese attack, and the sites of shell strikes became thronged by eager locals the next day. Photographers snapped pictures of '...children playing in a huge hole created by a shell outside a small grocery store in Woollahra'.[33] The economic effects of the Japanese bombardment were negligible, but demonstrated again the Japanese penchant for hit-and-run nuisance attacks using their submarines, all designed to lower civilian morale as well as cause physical damage to the enemy infrastructure and economy. Civilian morale was not lowered by the bombardment of Sydney, though many people still harboured fantasies of a Japanese invasion of Australia in the backs of their minds.

The bombardment of Sydney by the *I-24* occurred shortly after midnight on 8 June. Two hours later another Japanese submarine, the *I-21* under Commander Matsumura, surfaced at Stockton Bight, approximately six miles north-east of Newcastle. Matsumura's intention was identical to that of his colleague, Hanabusa, namely to bombard important shore targets vital to the Australian war economy. Matsumura's attack was to prove to be three times heavier than that launched upon Sydney on the same night, but on this occasion local Australian defences were able to reply, if ineffectually. In twenty minutes the *I-21* unleashed thirty-four shells from her deck-gun into the city of Newcastle, causing some damage, although once again the armour-piercing anti-ship ammunition used by the Japanese mainly failed to explode on contact with buildings and road surfaces and either ploughed through brick walls or buried themselves deep in the earth.

The Japanese were targeting Newcastle's B.H.P. steelworks and shipyards, but because of the range, darkness and the motion of the submarine on the surface of the sea, accuracy was difficult and shells ended up landing all over the city and in the sea. Newcastle was not blacked-out because no warning had been received by local civil defence authorities concerning an imminent attack, although as soon as the bombardment began local residents started to head for air raid shelters or their basements. The Japanese naval gunners had immediately to hand the twenty shells stored inside the ready-locker beside the deck-gun, and they also requested a further fourteen be brought topside during the engagement from the submarine's magazine below decks. Included in the thirty-four shells fired that night were eight star shells sent aloft to provide the Japanese with increased illumination to try to discern their targets and fall of shot, a local reporter noting inaccurately that 'Flare shells appeared in the sky over Newcastle before the explosions began'.[34]

The local defence of Newcastle was provided by the Fort Scratchley Battery located inside the fort of the same name on the shoreline, and by the Rail Battery, which consisted of a pair of First World War-vintage Hotchkiss 2-pounder emplaced field guns that protected the river mouth. Fort Scratchley's searchlights failed to pinpoint the *I-21* as she sailed closer to Newcastle, firing as she went, though the fort's gunners could clearly discern the submarine's deck-gun muzzle flashes every time she fired. It took the Fort Scratchley Battery thirteen minutes before they returned fire at the *I-21*, the battery's commanding officer, Captain Watson, roughing out a fairly accurate range and bearing on the Japanese submarine from the tell-tale flashes of her gun. A communications telephonist then reported, 'Fire Command says engage when ready, Sir!' Captain Watson is then reported to have said, 'Tell them I bloody well have!'[35] The big guns at Scratchley fired only four rounds in reply to the *I-21*'s thirty-four before the submarine made off. As the Japanese submarine manoeuvred and fired, the gunners in the fort had experienced trouble depressing their gun barrels sufficiently to engage the target, one of their four shots removing part of the roof of the Electricity Commission office building in the city.

Some of the Japanese shells fell harmlessly into the sea, some exploded on the surface in white plumes of water, while others remain on the seabed to this day, unexploded. Other shells crashed into buildings across the city. One landed next to the tram depot, another tore through a row of houses in Parnell Place, close to the fort. Another penetrated a storage shed at the

B.H.P. Steelworks (which was probably Matsumura's primary target), while yet another exploded at the Newcastle Ocean Baths, a swimming pool by the beach. With so much steel flying about it is a wonder that civilians were not killed or seriously injured. One soldier who had been asleep in the fort when the attack began leapt out of bed and twisted his ankle, and two civilians were injured by falling masonry in the city, but casualties remained negligible. The next day's addition of the *Newcastle Morning Herald* hailed 'The Luckiest Boy in Town', a story about a young boy and his brother who had been watching the action from their bedroom window at Parnell Place when the Fort Scratchley guns had opened fire close by. With ringing ears, the boys' mother herded them downstairs to the lounge, just as a Japanese shell had slammed through the window of the recently vacated bedroom, cut the boy's bed in two and set fire to the room's contents. Dozens of properties throughout Newcastle were left scarred by shrapnel, and a good many window panes were shattered or cracked by the concussions from the Fort Scratchley guns opening fire. It has been surmised that had the Japanese managed to land thirty-four conventional 140mm high explosive shells throughout Newcastle instead of the inappropriate anti-ship shells actually used, very considerable damage and loss of life would have occurred. The same can be said of the attack on Sydney, the Ellwood Oil Refinery bombardment in California on 17 February and the two attacks later in June on the Estevan Point lighthouse in Canada and Fort Stevens in Oregon. Fort Scratchley has gone down in history as the only Australian fort to engage an enemy surface target in wartime, and is now a museum. The *Newcastle Morning Herald* had much to say about the twin attacks on Sydney and Newcastle, most of it concerning the lessons to learned from such events:

> The reaction of Newcastle and Sydney to the raids and to the firing of East Coast batteries in anger for the first time in Australian history was one of curiosity mixed with irritation at the disturbance at a night's rest. Perhaps the enemy's attack was not so stupid as might appear. His purpose was intimidation. He was testing civilian nerves, and doubtless hoped by this demonstration that…he still has a number of submarines

off our coast to slow down production and to limit the use of our coastal waters. Its effect was to annoy, not frighten, civilians, and to hammer home…the need for vigilance, for increased production, and for lending every energy to the great task of keeping Australia free and restoring the freedom of the seas.[36]

The reporter perhaps summed up quite neatly the feelings of most Australians following the midget submarine attacks, and two recent gun bombardments:

If the Japanese planned to lower civilian morale, they succeeded only in disturbing a complacency of which we are well rid, and in spurring our determination to make an end of such impertinences, together with more serious affronts to our national pride and honour.[37]

Australia would not be frightened by the seeming impunity with which the Japanese were able to strike at the country. Indeed, the local newspaper warned the residents of Newcastle that one of the reasons the Japanese had been able to strike at the city was the lack of a 'brownout' during non-alert times. The newspaper commented that:

…the instinct…to switch on lights and watch the proceedings is potentially dangerous. Curiosity is natural, but it killed more than cats and it cannot be impressed too strongly on civilians that they will serve their own and the community's interests best by keeping lights off and going quietly to shelter.[38]

These were wise words for the Japanese planned to revisit the city to bombard it again.

The Japanese midget submarine attacks on shipping in Sydney Harbour, and the subsequent bombardment of the city's suburbs and the city of Newcastle by the large I-class submarines, was not part of an elaborate Japanese invasion plan. The Japanese never seriously considered invading the continent. At the time of the Japanese midget submarine attacks on Sydney Harbour, Australia appeared isolated and indeed in imminent danger. Darwin, Derby,

Katherine and Broome in the north had all suffered serious attention from Japanese bombers. Nearly every outpost of the British Empire in the Far East, Malaya, Hong Kong and Singapore to mention the most significant, had all fallen to the seemingly relentless Japanese war machine, and thousands of Australian servicemen had been taken prisoner. The fighting in New Guinea was fierce as Australian and Japanese troops fought each other, the jungle and disease along the Kokoda Trail. It was imperative that the Australians retained control of Port Moresby, and just as imperative for the Japanese to possess it. Certainly, the Japanese Navy was interested in isolating Australia by interdicting her merchant fleet, and by the aerial bombing of her northern towns and cities, but this strategy also became increasingly difficult following Japanese losses at the Battle of Midway in 1942. The myth that Australia was saved from a Japanese invasion by the fighting along the Kokoda Trail in New Guinea, or the Battle of the Coral Sea, are simply not supported by actual Japanese plans.

By early 1942, after the Japanese had invested the Netherlands East Indies (now Indonesia), Japan was within striking distance of the Australian mainland, and a few Japanese naval officers mooted a plan to extend the Empire's conquests onto the continent itself. The Imperial Japanese Army, however, immediately balked at such a plan, and killed it at the earliest possible opportunity. The army's reservations were not based on a lack of courage or ability, but rather on the very practical manpower problem they faced as the 'Greater East Asia Co-Prosperity Sphere' (the Japanese euphemism for their new empire in the Far East) rapidly expanded. The Japanese found themselves, by mid-1942, in a similar situation to Germany, fighting a war on two fronts.

After June 1941, approximately three-quarters of the German Army was fully occupied fighting the Soviets in European Russia, leaving the remainder to hold off the British and Americans elsewhere. So the Imperial Japanese Army faced an equal challenge, namely the occupation of eastern China and Manchuria, and constant war with the Chinese Nationalists and Communists on the one hand and total war against British, American, Australian, Dutch and New Zealand forces in the

Pacific and south-east Asia.

For Japan, the planned subjugation of China had been fully unleashed in 1937 when they had engineered an undeclared war, as prior to 1941 the army had most of its way in strategic planning. Japanese aggression in China properly began with the Manchurian Incident of September 1931, when the Japanese blew up a section of their railway in southern Manchuria and then blamed the Chinese. The Incident occurred at the town of Shenyang, then known as Mukden, and led to the Japanese occupation of Manchuria. After occupying the province the Japanese renamed it Manchukuo, and installed the last Emperor of China (who had been forced to abdicate in 1911), Pu Yi, as head of state in February 1932. Not satisfied with this, the Japanese then applied considerable pressure to the Chinese government to bow to its territorial demands, eventually growing tired of the politicking and engineering another 'incident' as a pretext for war. In July 1937 shots were exchanged between Japanese and Chinese soldiers at the Luguo Bridge (then known as the Marco Polo Bridge) in Beijing. The Japanese then went on to occupy Beijing and Tianjin (then known as Tientsin). The Chinese Nationalist leader Chiang Kai-shek refused to negotiate an end to hostilities on Japanese terms. After protracted fighting, the Japanese occupied Shanghai (minus the International Settlement and French Town settled by European and American citizens which was not occupied until December 1941), before capturing the national capital at Nanjing and committing one of the world's worst atrocities against a civilian population known as the 'Rape of Nanking' in which approximately 320,000 Chinese were exterminated. In late 1938, Hankou (Hankow) and Guangzhou (Canton) were taken, and the Nationalist Chinese retreated to a new temporary capital at Chongqing (Chungking), where the struggle was continued with Allied assistance along the Burma Road until 1945. The Second Sino-Japanese War saw two million Japanese soldiers in China, and this figure remained a constant throughout the Second World War. Even as the Japanese Empire was eroded by the American's island-hopping campaign across the Pacific, and the British and Commonwealth drive through Burma, a massive force had to be maintained in China, known as the Kwantung Army.

The Soviet Union continued to pose a threat to the Japanese occupation of Manchuria, which necessitated a large deterrent force besides the Kwantung Army facing the Chinese. Therefore, the army simply did not possess a sufficient stock of trained manpower in reserve to make the occupation of the huge Australian continent, or parts of it, feasible. The Imperial Japanese Navy also dismissed the idea of invading Australia, arguing that they possessed insufficient ships to conduct all of their operations across the Pacific and Indian Oceans. Prime Minister John Curtin and the Australian government knew of Japanese reservations concerning invading the continent from intelligence briefings derived from intercepted and decrypted Japanese radio traffic, but fear of an invasion served as a useful propaganda tool to rally the Australian people behind the war. Government posters were issued, one infamously proclaiming of the Japanese 'He's Coming South' to reinforce in the minds of ordinary Australians the grave danger they faced and the necessity of pulling together and supporting the war, and the Curtin government. Curtin and General Douglas MacArthur ('Dugout Doug' had been in Australia since being ordered out of the Philippines in March 1942 prior to the surrender of the Bataan Peninsula) had been informed of the Japanese abandonment of an invasion plan in early 1942, but Curtin withheld this information from the Australian people. The submarine attacks on Sydney and Newcastle in May only served to reinforce what Curtin had been warning, and it was only in mid-1943 that Curtin announced that no Japanese invasion was expected in the foreseeable future. Curtin was right in withholding this information, because the threat of invasion galvanized Australia to prosecute the war against Japan. The problem for historians has been the persuasiveness of Curtin's argument. He did such a thorough job of inculcating a belief in a planned Japanese invasion in the minds of Australians that this myth persists even today.

As for the submarines responsible for strengthening Curtin's hold over Australia, Hanabusa and the *I-24* struck again just after the sun rose on 9 June 1942, south-east of Jervis Bay. Launching a submerged attack on the British freighter *Orestes* (7,748-tons), both of the torpedoes that Hanabusa fired malfunctioned and blew up before reaching their target. Frustrated, the Japanese ordered his submarine to the surface, and he determined to sink the *Orestes* with his deck-gun. Unfortunately, although the crew banged away at the fast retreating freighter, they only scored a single hit that caused minimal damage, but they continued firing until Hanabusa ordered the attack halted and broke off contact with the freighter.

The *I-21* continued with her mission along the Australian coast well into June 1942. On 12 June the submarine was forty miles off Sydney when the lookouts spotted an eight-ship, lightly defended, coastal convoy. The convoy was proceeding from Newcastle to Whyalla. At 1.14 a.m. Commander Matsumura fired four torpedoes at the convoy, the spread designed to strike two of the eight ships making their way slowly along the coast. One of the torpedoes struck the 5,967-ton *Guatemala*, a Panamanian registered coke carrier that had been chartered by the Australian government. Within an hour the crew had taken to the boats and the *Guatemala* had sunk. Thereafter, the *I-21* headed for base, arriving at Kwajalein on 25 June before cruising to Japan for a major overhaul.

In all, the Eastern Advance Detachment sank six merchantmen during this operation, but the yield of these actions was disappointing. Too much effort had been expended at the outset in launching the unorthodox midget attacks. Also, many of the torpedoes had malfunctioned during the many attacks launched on merchant shipping. The Detachment failed in its most important mission of cutting the supply lines between Australia and its British and American allies. Once again, the Japanese submarine force had only partially succeeded in its allotted tasks, and had lost a great many well-trained and committed officers and men in the process.

Notes
1. Peggy Warner & Sadao Seno, *The Coffin Boats: Japanese Midget Submarine Operations in the Second World War*, (London: Leo Cooper), 1986, p.129
2. H. Tanaka, 'The Japanese Navy's operations against Australia in the Second World War, with a commentary on Japanese sources,' *Journal of the Australian War Memorial*, Issue 30, April 1997
3. Colin Smith, *Singapore Burning: Heroism and Surrender in World War II*,

(London: Penguin Books Ltd.), 2005, p.43

4. Tanaka, op. cit.

5. ibid.

6. *Japanese Midget Submarine Attack on Sydney Harbour, night of 31 May/1 June 1942. Reconstruction of events from Japanese and Australian Sources* by G. Hermon Gill, AWM54/622/5/8, (Australian War Memorial, Canberra)

7. ibid.

8. *Midget Submarine Attack on Sydney Harbour – Signal*s, B6121/161K, (National Archives of Australia, Canberra)

9. Gill, op. cit.

10. ibid.

11. ibid.

12. *Midget submarine attack on Sydney Harbour*, MP1049/5, 2026/21/79, (National Archives of Australia, Canberra)

13. Gill, op. cit.

14. ibid.

15. ibid.

16. Peggy Warner & Sadao Seno, *The Coffin Boats: Japanese Midget Submarine Operations in the Second World War*, (London: Leo Cooper), 1986, p.128

17. Andrew Mollo, *The Armed Forces of World War II*, (London: MacDonald & Co (Publishers) Ltd), 1981, p.252

18. Data derived from Bob Hackett & Sander Kingsepp's http://www.com-binedfleet.com/I-24.htm

19. ibid.

20. Data derived from Bob Hackett & Sander Kingsepp's http://www.com-binedfleet.com/I-27.htm

21. *Sydney Morning Herald*, 8 June 1942, front page

22. ibid.

23. ibid.

24. ibid.

25. Address by His Excellency Major General Michael Jeffrey AC CVO MC, Governor-General of the Commonwealth of Australia on the occasion of Warringah Australia Remembers Trust Commemorative Service to mark the 62nd anniversary of the defence of Sydney: Manly, New South Wales, 28 May 2004

26. Warner and Seno, op. cit., p.159

27. *Sydney Morning Herald*, 8 June 1942, front page

28. ibid.

29. ibid.

30. ibid.

31. ibid.

32. ibid.

33. Address by His Excellency Major General Michael Jeffrey AC CVO MC, Governor-General of the Commonwealth of Australia on the occasion of Warringah Australia Remembers Trust Commemorative Service to mark the 62nd anniversary of the defence of Sydney: Manly, New South Wales, 28 May 2004

34. *Sydney Morning Herald*, 8 June 1942, front page
35. The Hon. Danna Vale MP, Minister for Veterans' Affairs, Minister Assisting the Minister for Defence, at the Fort Scratchley Dedication Dinner at City Hall, Newcastle, 2002
36. *Newcastle Morning Herald*, 9 June 1942, front page
37. ibid.
38. ibid.

Chapter 7

Air Raid Oregon

In just a few more minutes you'll make history. You will be first person ever to bomb the mainland of America! If all goes well, Fujita, you will not be the last!

Lieutenant-Commander Meiji Tagami, *I-26*,
9 September 1942

Chief Warrant Officer (Flying) Nobuo Fujita was responsible for one of the truly audacious and risky plans of the Second World War. His plan demonstrated an awareness of the great potential Japanese submarines had over all the other submersibles in both Allied and Axis service. Japanese submarines were unique in that many carried an aircraft onboard. It was Fujita who turned the reconnaissance role of the Japanese submarine-based aircraft on its head and dreamed up a novel way to strike directly at the mainland of the United States.

   Fujita had been conscripted into the Imperial Japanese Navy in 1932. In 1933, at the age of twenty-two, he had been selected for training as a naval aviator and was evidently a natural flier for he was employed before hostilities in the dangerous occupation of test pilot. During the attack on Pearl Harbor on 7 December 1941 Fujita was serving as a pilot aboard the Junsen Type-B1 submarine *I-25*. This class of submarine was equipped with an E14Y1 reconnaissance floatplane, a rather flimsy but extremely useful contraption. The careful design of the floatplane, keeping size, speed and weight to a minimum, meant that the E14Y1 made an extremely useful addition to Japan's scouting submarine fleet. The aircraft, codenamed the 'Glen' by the Allies, was powered by a nine-cylinder, 340-horsepower Haitachi Tempu 12 radial engine generating a cruising speed of only eighty-five miles per hour. The aircraft was light, as it only weighed 3,500 pounds because it was constructed from a composite airframe of fabric-covered metal and wood.[1]If the aircraft was flown at the optimum cruising speed of eighty-five miles per hour the two-man crew could stay airborne for five hours and operate up to 200 miles from their 'mother' ship. The E14Y1, although primarily designed for reconnaissance work, could carry a maximum of 340-lbs of ordnance, consisting of incendiary and anti-personnel bombs, and it was this small bomb load capacity that interested Fujita. For defence against other aircraft the little floatplane was armed with a single 7.7mm machine gun operated by the observer from his position in the rear cockpit.

Fujita was supposed to have taken to the skies over Hawaii on 7 December, providing the fleet with additional reporting on the progress of the operation against the US Pacific Fleet, but due to the delicate nature of the E14Y1, he had to scrub his sortie because of slight damage to his aircraft when it was still aboard the *I-25*. Although Fujita was frustrated at not being able to take part in the operation against Pearl Harbor, whilst sitting out his enforced 'unemployment' as a pilot aboard the *I-25* an idea had sprung into his head regarding an offensive use for the E14Y1 floatplane. Fujita also had on his side the fact that he was an experienced pilot, and although not an officer, he was listened to within the confines of the *I-25*.

Fujita was required to pass his idea up through the chain of command, beginning with his executive officer aboard the *I-25*, Lieutenant Tatsuo Tsukudo. Tsukudo was impressed immediately by Fujita's suggestion, and he told him 'You ought to put your ideas in writing, Fujita, and forward them to the High Command'.[2] Inspired by this vote of confidence, Fujita duly sat down and wrote out a plan entirely of his own invention designed to strike directly at the mainland of the United States. The plan was developed around the use of a Type-B1 submarine, such as the *I-25*, and her onboard Yokosuka E14Y1 reconnaissance aircraft. Fujita planned to use the aircraft, suitably armed with bombs, to attack the vital Panama Canal, US Navy bases along the west coast, and aircraft production facilities, such as the giant Boeing plant in Seattle. The submarine would also attack enemy

142

shipping as the aerial operations were underway, extending the striking capability of the mission into a dual purpose offensive from the air and beneath the waves.

The skipper of the *I-25*, Lieutenant-Commander Meiji Tagami, endorsed Fujita's letter to headquarters, which meant that the 'Fujita Plan' would now reach the desks of senior officers able to divert the necessary resources to make it all a reality. Fujita was forced to wait for some time, and to continue with his duties aboard the *I-25* as the submarine patrolled off Australia and New Zealand during February and March 1942. Fujita's daring and flying skills were put to great use, as he took the E14Y1 up on reconnaissance flights over Sydney, Melbourne and Hobart in Australia, and Wellington and Auckland in New Zealand, demonstrating how easy it would be to drop bombs instead of taking photographs. By June the *I-25* was back off the American west coast, and as recounted in Chapter 5, the *I-25* had launched a deck-gun bombardment of Fort Stevens, on the coast of Oregon, on 21 June. Fujita had still not received word regarding his plan. But, by July 1942 the *I-25* had arrived back in Yokosuka, and Fujita found there was a message waiting for him on his arrival. He was ordered to report forthwith to the Naval General Staff's First Bureau (Operations) in Tokyo to attend a meeting.

After the discussion was wound up, Fujita was sworn to secrecy about the plan and told to report back to the *I-25*, which would be the designated submarine to undertake the mission. Commander Tagami was later briefed in secret, the priority being to get Fujita close enough to the enemy shore for the floatplane to make an impact. Fujita left navy headquarters stunned at the realization that his superiors had accepted a version of his own plan, and absolutely determined that the plan would be a success. With his tiny floatplane Chief Warrant Officer Fujita would set out to bring the long arm of Japanese destruction to Oregon, and, if all went well, reinforce in the American public's mind the fear that Japan was capable of striking at the mainland of the United States at will.

On 7 September the *I-25* arrived off the coast of Oregon, but Commander Tagami found the area unwelcoming with high seas and driving rain. He quickly realized that conditions were completely unsuitable for the launch of the floatplane and decided instead to wait out the bad weather. Stowed aboard the submarine were six 76-kg thermite aerial incendiary bombs, and Fujita planned to make three sorties to the American coast, dropping a brace of bombs on each occasion. When detonated, each bomb would scatter 520 incendiary pellets that burned at 2,700 degrees Fahrenheit, spreading over an area of 100 square yards. It was expected that if the six bombs were dropped at different points across the coastal forests, major conflagrations would be started that would soon burn out of control threatening property and lives, and spreading panic in their wake. The Japanese knew that September was considered a time of high fire risk in Oregon, though this year's weather turned out to be very different from most preceding years.

Eventually, on the early morning of 9 September, the sea conditions were right for the safe launch and recovery of the floatplane. The *I-25* was twenty-five miles west of the United States coast. Tagami requested Fujita's presence in the submarine's control room. He gestured towards the raised periscope and asked Fujita to take a look. 'Tell me what you think,' asked Tagami as Fujita peered intently through the eye-piece. Fujita turned away from the periscope and nodded his head, 'Captain,' he said, 'it looks good. I think we can do it today.' Tagami nodded in reply and a broad smile broke across his face. 'Fine,' a grinning Tagami replied, and then added to the already charged atmosphere inside the boat with a few well-chosen words. 'In just a few more minutes you'll make history. You will be first person ever to bomb the mainland of America! If all goes well, Fujita, you will not be the last!' Fujita bowed deeply and requested permission to prepare. Meeting Petty Officer Okuda, Fujita and his observer once again donned their flying suits, helmets and goggles, adjusting their automatic pistols carried on their belts in brown leather holsters. Fujita would also carry a samurai sword topside that would accompany him on the historic mission he was about to commence.

The *I-25* surfaced in the pre-dawn darkness, mechanics clattering topside to begin the familiar routine of assembling the floatplane. On this occasion armourers carefully positioned a pair of thermite incendiaries beneath the aircraft's wing pylons, arming them shortly before takeoff. The aircraft's radial engine roared into life, shattering the offshore silence, and with a wave of his hand Fujita, Okuda and the Yokosuka floatplane shot down the catapult runway along the submarine's deck and rose gracefully into the sky as the sun broke over the horizon. It appeared as a good omen to Fujita, as the Land of the Rising Sun sent two of its young men to bomb the United States. The time was 5.35 a.m. and history was indeed about to be made.

Fujita would once again use lighthouses as convenient navigational markers on his trip to the Oregon coast, as he had done during his reconnaissance missions over Australia earlier in the year, turning the aircraft north-east towards the light at Cape Blanco. On reaching the lighthouse Fujita banked towards the south-east and prepared to commence bombing.

At the Port Orford Coast Guard Station Seaman Second Class Ezra Ross was on duty. Ross heard the Japanese aircraft pass overhead and thought the sound of the engine strange and unfamiliar. The engine certainly did not sound like any American aircraft he had heard over the area before. Unable visually to identify the strange intruder, Ross informed the US Army Air Corp's IV Fighter Command of his suspicions, and they began to track the unidentified aircraft on radar while also informing 4th Air Force headquarters in San Francisco. Fujita was on a course that would take the two Japanese airmen to Mount Emily, inside Siskiyou National Forest. US Forest Service personnel manned a series of towers across the area, where many acted as fire wardens and others had been retrained as air defence observers to assist the army in protecting the coastal areas in the seemingly unlikely event of enemy aerial incursion. These civil defence personnel relied on the visual identification of aircraft, and were able to communicate any sightings to IV Fighter Command to investigate.

Mount Emily is about fifty miles from the coast, and as the little Japanese floatplane headed towards its target it was spotted and reported several times by civil defence workers. Fujita flew close to the Mount Emily lookout, the noise of the aircraft's engine causing fire warden Howard Gardner to step outside and peer skyward. A thin fog hung over the forest, but Gardner was able to make out a small aircraft gently circling the area. Thinking it was suspicious, Gardner went back inside and radioed the ranger headquarters at Gold Beach, thirty-miles north of the small town of Brookings. Another firewatcher, a university student named Keith Johnson, was busy clearing forest trails close to another tower located at Bear Wallow, seven miles east of Mount Emily. His attention was also drawn to the unfamiliar engine noise in the sky, but the fog prevented him seeing anything and he soon forgot about it and returned to his work. At Long Ridge, thirty miles from Brookings, husband and wife air defence observers Ed and Esther Conley were manning their tower in the forest when they clearly discerned Fujita's aircraft. The Conley's report was passed to IV Fighter Command, which was beginning to realize that something unusual was occurring. Indeed, the Conleys' prompt report later brought them an official commendation from Brigadier General Barney M. Giles, commander of the 4th Air Force.[3]

As Fujita circled just above the light fog in the early morning light, he judged himself to be over the target, fifty miles inland in an area of dense forest. He released one of his two bombs, and both Okuda and he peered intently over the side of their aircraft to observe the result. The bomb impacted the forest floor and exploded in a brilliant white flash, and before Fujita flew on both men observed flames flickering through the trees below them. In Fujita's mind his plan was working, and he flew on to deposit his second bomb five miles from the first, observing another successful impact detonation as the bomb showered the surrounding woodland with hundreds of incendiary pellets. Gardner, from his position at Mount Emily, had observed the Japanese aircraft at 6.24 a.m. Around noon, and long after the Japanese aircraft had left the scene, Gardner, from the top of his tower, noticed a thin column of smoke rising from the forest to the south-east. He reported this to Gold Beach, and his superiors immediately ordered him to strike out on foot and investigate the suspected fire. Keith Johnson had, by noon, returned to his observation tower from his morning's work, and ranger headquarters radioed him with instructions to conduct a careful binocular observation of the surrounding forest. Johnson soon discovered the same plume of black smoke rising into the still midday air and, on confirming Gardner's report to headquarters, Johnson was ordered out on foot to assist him. When Gardner and Johnson arrived at the source of the smoke they discovered a sixty-foot wide circle of forest had been incinerated, and at its centre was a small crater. Strewn about the scorched forest floor were metal fragments and strange pellet-shaped objects. The two wardens began to gather up some of this material, and at 4.20 p.m. Gold Beach received a report from the two men of suspected bomb damage in the forest at Mount Emily.

Fujita, believing that his first attack on the United States had been successful, now headed back at low level for the *I-25*. On the return flight Fujita and Okuda spotted two merchant ships steaming in company north up the coast, and to avoid being seen Fujita changed his course to north-north-east before relocating the submarine. He landed the aircraft in the sea and taxied alongside the submarine where crew and plane were winched safely aboard by crane. Mechanics busily completed the disassembly and stowage of the E14Y1 and the submarine submerged.

The next day, while still in the same area, lookouts positioned on the *I-25*'s conning tower gave a cry of alarm. They had spotted a lone plane bearing down on their submarine from the land. 4th Air Force had scrambled several aircraft to investigate the reports received of an unidentified plane in the vicinity of Mount Emily and Brookings, and by sheer luck a Lockheed A-29 Hudson bomber of the 42nd Bomb Group flying out of McChord Field found the *I-25* sitting on the surface off the Oregon coast. As the American aircraft dived in to attack Tagami ordered an immediate crash-dive. The A-29 released three 300-pound depth charges over the submerged submarine, by which time the *I-25* was at a depth of 230 feet. The first depth charge exploded at eighty feet, and the other two at 100. The *I-25* was violently shaken by the detonations, and Tagami took his boat down to the seabed west of Port Orford.[4] The *I-25* had sustained some minor damage, including a damaged antenna lead and the radio room had sprung a leak, but otherwise his boat and crew were unharmed and the mission would continue. The Hudson bomber dropped seven more depth charges to no effect. Four thermite incendiaries remained aboard the *I-25* awaiting delivery to the United States by Fujita and Okuda.

Forestry workers Gardner and Johnson camped overnight at the site of their discovery of bomb damage in the forest, and the next day, 10 September, two other wardens, who had been sent to assist them, arrived at the scene. Between them the four men collected sixty-five pounds of man-made material from the site and this evidence was immediately rushed to waiting army intelligence personnel at Brookings for analysis. An FBI agent arrived at Brookings to assist the army, and it was not very long before metal fragments from the bomb's case revealed the weapon's Japanese origin. With the verbal reports of various fire wardens and air defence observers of an unidentified aircraft over the national forest on 9 September, and the Hudson's attack on a Japanese submarine the day after, the 'Fujita Plan' revealed itself to the American authorities. The worry for the army and the FBI was when and where would the Japanese strike again? They also swiftly realized the lucky escape Oregon had had, as neither bomb had caused large fires. When the *I-25* had been waiting out the bad weather submerged off the Port Orford Heads for several days in early September, rain and fog had repeatedly soaked the forests, and the dampness that remained when Fujita attacked on 9 September prevented either of the fires he had started from taking hold among the trees. The Americans would probably not have nature on their side again if the Japanese mounted similar attacks in the near future.

The United States government attempted to withhold news of the daring Japanese raid from the American people, anxious to prevent a panic and to reassure them that the west coast was adequately defended. However, the authorities almost immediately lost control of the story. This was because dozens of service and civilian personnel had been involved in the events of 9–10 September, and many had talked openly about them to one another and their families. It was not long before the newspapers had the story, fuelling calls for increased defences along the west coast to prevent this kind of thing from occurring again. In the same way that the May 1942 midget submarine attacks on Sydney Harbour had unsettled the Australian people, fuelling widely held, though ultimately false, invasion fears and a feeling of vulnerability, so Fujita's attack caused considerable disquiet throughout the western United States. The American authorities

148

took some steps towards allaying public anxiety. Firstly, a stricter blackout was enforced along the west coast in the hope of denying the Japanese navigational points when launching their 'sneak' attacks, although someone decided not to include light-houses as part of the blackout because of their vital importance to coastal shipping and the fishing fleets. This would prove to be a mistake, as Fujita was able to utilize a lighthouse once again during his second air raid on Oregon. The FBI went so far as to conduct detailed searches of some of the quiet north-western lakes, harbouring suspicions that the Japanese could have been basing floatplane bombers in them. Naturally, these searches turned up nothing of Japanese origin. The state of Washington was sent four further fighter aircraft to stiffen its coastal defences, though these planes were later removed when no further Japanese attacks occurred after the end of September 1942.

Aboard the *I-25* enthusiasm still dominated the submarine's atmosphere. Fujita was satisfied that the 9 September raid had been successful, although he had no way of knowing the extent of the blazes started by his incendiary bombs in the forests around Mount Emily. He and Petty Officer Okuda, his observer, were satisfied that some damage had been inflicted on the United States as both men had seen the thermite incendiary bombs explode on the forest floor, and had observed flames on the ground among the trees before they had flown away from the scene.

There remained stored aboard the *I-25* four more 76-kg incen-diary bombs, sufficient ordnance for two further air raids on the United States. Lieutenant-Commander Tagami, skipper of the *I-25*, was happy to allow Fujita to launch a second raid, suggesting helpfully that, 'We'll make the next one a night attack, Fujita, for the Americans will be expecting another sunrise one.' Shortly after midnight on 29 September the *I-25* quietly surfaced about fifty miles west of the Cape Blanco lighthouse on the coast of Oregon. Once again, the familiar routine of assembling and arming the Yokosuka floatplane was conducted, until permission was received to launch the aircraft on its mission. Tagami ordered his executive officer, Lieutenant Tatsuo Tsukudo, to turn the submarine's bows into the wind, and then the catapult was fired and Fujita and Okuda hurtled along the deck and rose gracefully into the night sky. The crewmen on deck stood silently, listening as the little aircraft droned away into the darkness.

The exclusion of lighthouses from the west coast blackout meant that Fujita was able to fly due east, using the Cape Blanco light to make landfall, and then he simply flew inland on the same heading for a further thirty minutes before releasing both of his bombs over the forests. At 5.22 a.m. a work gang of forestry personnel reported to their Gold Beach headquarters by radio that they had heard an unidentified aircraft pass overhead. At that time the men were about seven miles east of Port Orford at a ranger station called Grassy Knob. It was immediately suspected that a Japanese aircraft had penetrated United States airspace again, and Ranger Headquarters instructed the men to conduct a ground search for forest fires as soon as it was light. Several fire-prevention patrols struck out into the forest at sun-up, but no one found anything suspicious. Fujita later stated that he had seen once again the brilliant white flash of a detonating incendiary bomb on both occasions that night when he had released them, but any blazes that did occur were small and burned themselves out before being seen by the firewatchers. Indeed, no fragments or incendiary pellets have ever been found from the Japanese bombs dropped on 29 September, and their remains are to this day somewhere on the forest floor, lost to time.

After releasing his bombs Fujita did not remain in the area but immediately turned his aircraft around and retraced his course to the coast, flying low past the Cape Blanco lighthouse and disappearing out to sea. Fujita visually relocated the *I-25* by following an oil slick that the submarine was trailing (possibly from damage caused by the Hudson maritime bomber's attack of 10 September). His plane was hastily hoisted aboard and disassembled, and then the *I-25* submerged. Fujita began immediate planning for a final sortie, as two thermite incendiary bombs still remained aboard the submarine. Once again, in a replay of the events that had delayed Fujita's first raid over the United States, rough weather and a thick sea mist closed in on the area preventing any launch of the floatplane. For several days the *I-25* hung around the area, both Tagami and Fujita hoping that the weather would clear sufficiently to allow the third and last sortie of the mission to be launched. However, the weather stubbornly refused to improve, and eventually Tagami decided to abandon any further efforts to launch Fujita and Okuda on a third air raid, and to concentrate instead on interdicting coastal shipping using the submarine. It was a frustrating end to Fujita's mission, a mission dogged by bad weather that had worked well to protect the forests of the Pacific Northwest from harm on two occasions.

On 4 October 1942 the *I-25* was sitting on the surface off the south Oregon coast charging her batteries. Commander Tagami had finally cancelled further floatplane sorties over the mainland of the United States for good owing to the deteriorating weather conditions at sea, which would have endangered both aircraft and crew in the launch and recovery of the E14Y1. However, Tagami was not intent on returning to Japan just yet, for as well as the two unused 76kg thermite incendiary bombs in storage, he still had six torpedoes aboard the *I-25*, and the determination to see them expended to maximum effect.

All remained quiet aboard the submarine, as she rolled in the heavy swell, her lookouts pensively scanning the horizon and the sky for both threats and opportunities. Their patience was rewarded when an opportunity presented itself in the form of the 6,653-ton American tanker *Camden*. Tagami immediately ordered 'General Quarters! Action stations!' and the boat moved to line up for a shot at the zigzagging tanker. Two Long Lance torpedoes shot from the *I-25*'s bow tubes, but the *Camden* successfully managed to evade both of them, and then made off at full speed in an attempt to outrun the submarine. The *I-25* gave a dogged pursuit, trailing the *Camden* for four hours until, off Coos Bay Tagami was able to move into another good firing position. A further torpedo hammered its way through the sea, impacting the *Camden* in the bows, which were rapidly enveloped by flames and dense smoke. The tanker shuddered and began to lose speed. Tagami was satisfied that the *Camden* was as good as lost, and he did not linger to witness the vessel's death throes.

The fire started by the Japanese torpedo strike began to spread through the *Camden*, and the captain ordered his crew off the stricken vessel in the lifeboats. The following day, the abandoned *Camden* was discovered to be still afloat, and the fire that had appeared to signal the end of the vessel had burned itself out. There was some hope that the vessel could be saved, and the tug

Kenai arrived to take the damaged tanker in tow. Hopes of salvaging her faded on 10 October when fire, which had burned down but had not completely extinguished, once again broke out and the tug slipped the towlines as the *Camden* succumbed to her mortal wound. The tanker finally went down in the mouth of the Columbia River.

In the meantime, the *I-25* had changed position to an area off Cape Sebastian, and Tagami kept his submarine sitting boldly on the surface as he searched out a new target. Three torpedoes were loaded and ready to fire, and all that was required was a little luck in finding a vessel to expend some on. Ironically, on 6 October, lookouts located the 7,038-ton tanker *Larry Doheny*, the same vessel Lieutenant-Commander Kozo Nishino had attacked but failed to destroy in his submarine the *I-17* on 23 December 1941. On this occasion Tagami would succeed where Nishino had failed, although the captain of the *Larry Doheny* attempted a fight back to save his vessel. The *I-25* stalked the *Larry Doheny* for ten minutes, carefully manoeuvring for a shot, Tagami aware that he only had the three torpedoes remaining aboard. After the firing position was achieved to his satisfaction Tagami ordered a single torpedo launched, and it appeared a foregone conclusion that the *Larry Doheny* would be struck. However, the wily skipper of the tanker abruptly altered course, deftly avoiding the running torpedo, and pointing his bows directly at the Japanese submarine, he ploughed at full speed towards a shocked collection of Japanese officers standing on the conning tower, determined to ram and sink the *I-25* with the great mass of his ship. Ramming was virtually the only offensive option open to a merchant captain when confronted with an enemy submarine, and on several occasions during the Second World War German and Japanese submarines were destroyed or severely damaged in this manner, although normally the vessel performing the ramming was a warship. Tagami now ordered another torpedo fired from practically point blank range. The torpedo closed the gap between the *I-25* and the charging tanker in only eighteen seconds, striking and detonating inside the *Larry Doheny*. Lookouts and officers on the submarine's conning tower dived for cover as smouldering shards of tanker and torpedo showered down all around them. The *Larry Doheny* heeled over and began immediately to sink by the head, Tagami allowing most of his crewmen the opportunity to view the ship's foundering through the submarine's periscope. After a few minutes the *I-25* departed the area at full speed on the surface, Tagami and his crew jubilant with their two successes over two days.[5]

Commander Tagami's sinking of the *Camden* and the *Larry Doheny* were the final successful submarine attacks made against shipping off the United States west coast during the Second World War. However, it was not the last act in the story of the *I-25*'s mission to America. On 10 October, and with just one torpedo remaining aboard, Tagami set a course for Japan and began the journey home for a refit and rest. On his way home he was almost responsible for a diplomatic incident between Japan and the Soviet Union. On the 11th the *I-25*'s lookouts reported, in heavy weather, what appeared to them to be two battleships moving in the direction of San Francisco. As the big Japanese submarine powered through the waves Tagami and his officers strained to make out exactly what kind of enemy vessels they had encountered, and were eventually rewarded by the sight of two submarines motoring in company on the surface. Tagami immediately, and logically, identified them as American submarines, and prepared to attack. On this occasion he decided upon a submerged attack, and with a rush of compressed air the last torpedo hammered away through the water towards one of the medium-sized, grey-painted submarines he could clearly see through his attack periscope. Thirty tense seconds passed, as Lieutenant Tsukudo's stopwatch recorded the torpedoes run through the water, when suddenly deep, powerful explosions reverberated through the *I-25*'s pressure hull indicating that the torpedo had found its mark. After noting another successful kill in his log, Tagami turned the *I-25* for home, arriving at Yokosuka on 24 October. Tagami had definitely sunk a submarine, but not an American vessel. His victim was the *L-16*, a 1,039-ton minelaying submarine belonging to the Red Navy. Skippered by Commander Dmitri Gussarov, the *L-16* was travelling in company with the *L-15*, both boats heading for San Francisco. They had departed from Petropavlovsk in Siberia and called in at Dutch Harbor in the Aleutian Islands before attempting to complete the final leg of their journey to California. The *L-15* attempted to attack the submerged *I-25* after spotting the Japanese submarine's periscopes above the surface of the water. The Soviet submarine managed to fire five rounds from her 45mm deck-gun at the periscopes, but they all landed harmlessly in the ocean around the *I-25* before the Japanese submarine made off and resumed her course for home.

Japan and the Soviet Union had maintained an uneasy peace along the Manchuria-Siberia border since the Soviets had checked Japanese moves to extend their conquests into Mongolia and Siberia at the Battle of Halkin Gol between May and September 1939. The Japanese had subsequently turned their expansionist attentions to dominating the Pacific and south-east Asia, as well as maintaining their hold over huge swathes of China. Although the Japanese had negotiated a non-aggression pact with Stalin in 1941, neither side trusted the other, and Japan stationed thousands of troops on the border as a deterrent to Soviet expansion. Having so many troops tied up so effectively and doing nothing was to seriously hamper Japan's ability to prosecute the war elsewhere. By 1942, and the *I-25*'s sinking of a Soviet submarine, the Japanese were fighting the United States in the Pacific, Britain, her empire and dominions in Burma, and also garrisoning vast areas of China. If Japan had been held responsible for the loss of a Soviet submarine and fifty sailors lives Stalin could have torn up the 1941 Pact and attempted to have snatched the resources of Manchuria for his own war machine. On this occasion the *I-25* was not identified, so no one was held responsible and the Pact remained in force. Only in the dying days of the Second World War in 1945 did Stalin unleash his forces upon the understrength Japanese Kwantung Army in Manchuria and Korea, achieving an extensive breakthrough ten days before Japan surrendered unconditionally to the Allies.

In 1962, Nobuo Fujita, by now a metals salesman in Japan, received a surprise invitation from a local community group in the United States called the Brookings Jaycees. Twenty years had passed since Fujita had piloted the tiny Yokosuka floatplane close to the town of Brookings in his attempt to set Oregon alight, and he was surprised to be asked to visit the town he had tried so hard to destroy. Fujita was also not a little suspicious as to why the

Americans would invite their former enemy to visit the site of his darkest hour. When the Japanese government was informed of the invitation to Fujita from Brookings, officials wrote to the town fathers wanting a reassurance that Fujita was not being lured to the United States to be tried as a war criminal!

It is clear from Fujita's later actions that his attempt to set the vast redwood forests of Oregon on fire in 1942, and to destroy dozens of towns and settlements, had weighed heavily on his conscience in the intervening two decades. He was determined to accept the invitation from the Jaycees, and to make an attempt at reconciliation with the Americans. Of course, not every inhabitant of Brookings was keen to see Fujita in the flesh, but Fujita tried hard to win everyone over. One of his first acts on arrival in the town was to present the mayor with a 400-year old samurai sword, a valuable family heirloom and the same sword that he had carried in the cockpit of his Yokosuka floatplane both times he had bombed Oregon. Fujita donated the weapon as a symbol of his heartfelt wish to atone for his wartime actions. The 'Fujita Sword', as it has become known, now resides on display inside the Chetco Public Library in Brookings, as a reminder of both Fujita's apology and of the bond which subsequently grew up between the wartime Japanese pilot and the citizens of a small Oregon town.

Fujita was a regular visitor to Brookings over the next thirty-five years, even bringing his granddaughter with him on occasions. He was responsible for creating a fund at the local library to educate the children of Brookings about other cultures, and he visited the site of one of his incendiary bomb strikes and planted a redwood sapling to atone for his actions. Fujita's willingness and apparent personal need to assist the community of Brookings extended to sponsoring local high school students' exchange programmes to Japan, as well as offering each student an all expenses paid tour of his country, the money for this coming each time out of his own pocket. Fujita eventually came to be held in such high esteem by Brookings that shortly before his death from lung cancer at the age of eighty-six in 1997 a representative from the town travelled to Japan to present him with a certificate confirming him as an 'Honorary Citizen' of Brookings. It was a fitting end to an extraordinary journey undertaken by Fujita when he first stood in the conference room in Tokyo in 1942, proud of his idea and so keen to make his plan a reality.

Notes
1. William H. Langenberg, 'Japanese Bomb the West Coast, *Aviation History*, November 1998
2. ibid.
3. Port Orford Historical Society, Oregon
4. Mark Felton, *Yanagi: The Secret Underwater Trade Between Germany and Japan, 1942–1945*, (Barnsley: Pen & Sword Maritime), 2005, pp.189-91
5. ibid.

Chapter 8

An Overview of Japanese Submarine Operations off Australia during 1943

That's right girlies, jump for it now.
Colonel Manson to Australian nurses aboard the *Centaur*,
14 May 1943

The Japanese never again mounted the kind of coordinated submarine attacks on Australia witnessed during mid-1942, when the Eastern Advance Detachment launched the midget attacks on Sydney Harbour and also bombarded the Sydney suburbs and the city of Newcastle. However, the Japanese did not entirely disappear from the waters around the continent, and several submarines were dispatched to harass coastal shipping and convoys throughout 1943. The submarines operated individually, and although they sank or damaged several Allied ships, their collective impact on the Australian war machine was slight, really constituted no more than a series of nuisance attacks designed to demonstrate a continued Japanese ability to strike at the Australian home front. Australian anti-submarine defences continued to develop, based on the fast corvettes, and Japanese submarine skippers became increasingly wary of the types of bold attacks they had made earlier in the war. The change in Australian naval tactics with the introduction of convoys in 1941 also had an effect on the effectiveness of Japanese submarines. Only six ships were sunk and two damaged by Japanese submarine attacks on convoys, while roving Japanese boats between 1941 and 1944 successfully destroyed eighteen ships that were travelling unescorted, proving the value of the convoy system.

The experienced *I-21*, famous for bombarding Newcastle in

157

1942, was to achieve a string of successes along the Australian coast during January and February 1943. Commander Matsumura took his boat out from the Japanese base at Rabaul on her fourth war patrol on 7 January, bound for the busy waters off Australia's east coast. By the 15th the *I-21* had arrived off Sydney and continued her patrol into the Tasman Sea off New South Wales where she achieved her first kill of the patrol on the 18th. Many vessels were still to be found sailing unescorted along the Australian coast, particularly smaller vessels plying the coastal trade routes, and these had always been a submariner's targets of choice. Submarine skippers viewed these unprotected ships as easy prey, as they would not have to avoid a sudden corvette or destroyer counter-attack, and, as long as the submarine attacked swiftly and devastatingly, it was unlikely that help would arrive before the stricken merchantman was finished off.

The small 2,051-ton Australian freighter *Kalingo* had departed from Sydney and was setting out across the Pacific for Plymouth in New Zealand when Matsumura came upon her on 18 January. Attacking while submerged, two torpedoes were fired at the *Kalingo*, which was critically damaged. Matsumura then surfaced and in a humanitarian gesture not usually demonstrated by officers of the Imperial Navy, he gave the crew of the freighter sufficient time to take to the ship's lifeboats before moving in to finish the vessel off. Once the merchantman's crew were safely out of harm's way, the *I-21* launched a third torpedo which hastened the end of the *Kalingo*, and Matsumura departed from the scene triumphant.

Matsumura's days work was not done, however, and later that evening a far more substantial target presented itself. This was the huge American tanker *Mobilube*, which had a small escort ship assigned to protect her. At 9.50 p.m. two torpedoes were unleashed towards the 10,222-ton ship, but the huge detonation of at least one strike failed to sink the tanker. Ignoring the escort vessel for the time being, Matsumura ordered his boat to the surface, and the deck-gunners began banging away at the huge tanker, until her escort returned their fire which forced the *I-21* back beneath the waves in a crash-dive. As Matsumura guided his boat out of danger, the escort dumped a pattern of six depth charges over the spot where the Japanese submarine had disap-

158

peared, but although the Japanese sailors were jolted about by the sonic detonations, their vessel escaped any damage and Matsumura made off confident that the *Mobilube* had been fatally wounded. Indeed, his assumption of another victory was correct, for although the great tanker was towed into port she was declared a total loss and later cut up for scrap.

The hunting off New South Wales, along the shipping lanes fanning out from Sydney, was to continue to provide Matsumura and the *I-21* with plenty of interdiction opportunities. The *I-21* crippled an American Liberty ship, the *Peter H. Burnett*, on 22 January, firing two torpedoes while at periscope depth. One struck home, severely damaging the vessel. As the *I-21* departed from the scene the American escort USS *Zane* and an Australian, HMAS *Mildura*, towed the vessel into Sydney where the ship's cargo of wool and mail were salvaged. The *Peter H. Burnett* was declared a total loss and met the same fate as the *Mobilube* in a breaker's yard reduced to scrap.[1]

As well as attacking Allied ships along the coast of New South Wales, the *I-21* was also detailed to conduct a reconnaissance of the coastline. Once again, the usefulness of the Yokosuka E14Y1 floatplane proved its worth, and Warrant Officer (Flying) Susumu Ito carried out a successful flight over Sydney Harbour on the night of 25 January. Ito reported the presence of at least one heavy cruiser and ten smaller warships inside the harbour. On 30 January Matsumura launched a single torpedo at a small British merchantman, the 1,036-ton *Giang Ann*, and would almost certainly have sunk her but for a torpedo malfunction. The torpedo began its run smoothly, but then detonated prematurely, allowing the British ship time to escape any further attention from the Japanese submarine. Matsumura was nothing if not bold, and on 8 February he located a convoy of ten ships off Montague Island. Convoy OC68 was making its way from Whyalla to Newcastle, and Matsumura scored an immediate hit on the lead ship, the 4,812-ton *Iron Knight*, a British ship carrying a cargo of iron ore. The torpedo strike under the bridge on the starboard side was so devastating that the *Iron Knight* went down like a stone in under two minutes, giving the crew virtually no time to abandon her. The Free French destroyer *Le Triomphant*, one of the convoy escorts, pulled fourteen survivors from off a floating life raft. Two days later off Port Macquarie Matsumura launched a spread of four torpedoes at the 7,176-ton American Liberty ship *Starr King*. This was an important prize to sink for the *Starr King* was loaded down with 7,000 tons of supplies destined for the US Army fighting the Japanese in New Caledonia. She was struck by two of the Japanese torpedoes, but did not sink immediately. The Australian escort vessel HMAS *Warramunga* rushed alongside the stricken freighter and took off the surviving members of her crew, and then attempted to take the *Starr King* in tow to hopefully prevent her loss. However, the freighter started to founder, and the commanding officer of the *Warramunga* ordered the tow lines severed, and the crew watched helplessly as the *Starr King* and all of her valuable supplies were swallowed up by the ocean.[2]

Ito took to the skies once again over the Australian coast on 19 February, the sortie proving a success despite his aircraft being detected by Australian radar. Whether the photographs his observer took were of any military value is questionable, but the fact that Ito's aircraft was not challenged in so sensitive an area for the second occasion during the submarine's patrol, and in an area that had already witnessed extensive Japanese submarine and aerial activity, indicated that the Australians still had some way to go to secure this particular stretch of coastline from enemy infiltration. Thereafter, Matsumura headed for Japan as his boat was in need of an overhaul after extensive operations so far from base, and the *I-21* concluded her war patrol at the giant Yokosuka Naval Base south of Tokyo on 3 March.

As Matsumura headed in to Japan to celebrate his most successful war patrol to Australia, another large I-boat was headed in the opposite direction. This was the *I-26*, under Commander Yokota. His mission was the same as that of his colleague Matsumura, with the exception of not launching any photographic reconnaissance sorties. The *I-26* was not nearly as successful as Matsumura's recent run along the New South Wales coast. On 11 April the *I-26* was nineteen miles off Cape Howe, Victoria, when her lookouts spotted Convoy QC86, which was making its way from Whyalla to Newcastle. Yokota struck and sank with torpedoes a Yugoslavian ship, the 4,732-ton *Recina*. She was carrying a cargo of iron ore, and was under Australian government charter. There followed for the *I-26* a period of

160

inaction, as no targets presented themselves until 24 April. Then, when thirty-five miles east of Bowen the *I-26* found a lone ship and attacked her. The Australian *Kowarra* (2,125-tons) was heading from Bowen to Brisbane loaded down with sugar, and she sank quickly after a single Japanese torpedo strike. This was Yokota's second and final kill of the patrol, and he headed back to base at Truk undoubtedly frustrated that more targets and opportunities had eluded his search.

The Type KD7 submarine *I-177* under the command of Lieutenant-Commander Hajime Nakagawa left Truk on its first war patrol on 10 April 1943 in company with sister submarines *I-178* and *I-180*. All were bound for the east coast of Australia, favoured hunting ground of the Imperial Navy's submarines. On 26 April the *I-177* was twenty miles south-east of Cape Byron, close to the city of Brisbane, when she encountered an escorted convoy. Moving quickly into an attack position, Nakagawa managed to sink the 8,724-ton British freighter *Limerick*, and also to avoid two depth charges dropped by the convoy escorts. On the same day Lieutenant-Commander Toshio Kusaka aboard the *I-180* also launched an attack on an unidentified merchant-man, but the freighter escaped and Kusaka end up wasting three of his torpedoes. The following day the *I-178*, under Commander Hidejiro Utsuki, was 100 miles off Port Stephens. Utsuki attacked and sank an American Liberty ship, the 7,176-ton *Lydia M. Childs*, which was loaded with tanks. However, on this occasion the RAAF attempted to take some measure of revenge against the Japanese submarine, a Catalina flying boat launching three bombing runs over the *I-178* an hour after she had sunk the Liberty. The *I-178* escaped without suffering any damage and made it unscathed back to Truk on 18 May.

During May 1943 the Australian army was heavily engaged against the Japanese on the island of Papua New Guinea. Fierce battles had raged at Buna, Gona and Sanananda, necessitating the evacuation of wounded soldiers to Australia for more extensive medical treatment. The *Centaur*, a large motor passenger ship, had undergone conversion into a hospital ship earlier in 1943, which had involved a radical alteration of not just her internal compartments, but also in her outward appearance. When the vessel left Sydney harbour on 12 May bound for Port Moresby in

New Guinea, she was painted a brilliant white, with thick green stripes running the length of her hull broken by huge red crosses. On her bows was painted the number '47', providing information that any enemy submarine skipper could investigate to determine the ship's identity and purpose. The number was the *Centaur*'s registration lodged with the International Red Cross in Switzerland, the IRC having informed the Japanese government of the ship's new role as a non-combatant vessel protected by International Law from any kind of attack. Although Japan had not signed the 1929 Geneva Conventions, she had nonetheless agreed prior to the outbreak of war to abide by the provisions concerning non-combatant status, and the rules regarding hospital ships that had been established as long ago as 1907.

The *Centaur*'s first task was to sail from Sydney to Cairns through Australian coastal waters regularly patrolled by Japanese submarines, and thence on to Port Moresby to collect wounded. Aboard her for the journey to New Guinea were sixty-four medical staff, including twelve Australian Army Medical Service nurses, who would stay on the ship to treat the wounded, and the 149 men, plus an additional forty-four attached personnel, of the 2/12th Field Ambulance who would be landed at Port Moresby to provide casualty clearing stations and aid posts for the front-line fighting troops. The *Centaur* had a crew of seventy-five men of the Merchant Navy, giving a total aboard of 332 souls all headed north into the war zone.[3]

The captain of the *Centaur* was sailing directly into seas where Japanese submarines had been recently operating and sinking Allied ships, trusting in his ship's clearly marked non-combatant status for protection. He was aware that the Japanese had been informed of his ship's status as a hospital vessel on 5 February, and he knew that their superiors would have apprised any roving submarine skippers of this fact. With hindsight, it is possible to see that the disaster that followed occurred as a result of a Japanese unwillingness to follow any rules concerning conduct in war, other than their own military code. The track record of the Japanese army and navy in conducting war since 1937 in China and throughout the Pacific and south-east Asia after 1941 was a litany of atrocities and flagrant breaches of internationally agreed codes of military and naval conduct, even those rules to which

Japan was bound or had agreed to honour. Put simply, the Japanese left much of the observance of these rules to individual commanders, who reacted depending upon the situation they faced, or the degree to which any such rules meant anything to them. The Japanese officer corps was renowned for being obsessively loyal to the Emperor to the ignorance of everything else, and slavishly obedient to the Bushido code of feudal Japan that took no account of prisoners or non-combatants within its ethos. Many officers were simply brutal and very often what we might subsequently define as sadistic in dealing with the enemies of Japan, and the *Centaur* was about to run foul of one the navy's most brutal submarine skippers. Lieutenant-Commander Hajime Nakagawa was on his first war patrol to Australian waters as commanding officer of the submarine *I-177*, a KD7 type completed in December 1942. Nakagawa, along with submarines *I-178* and *I-180*, formed Submarine Division 22, 3rd Submarine Squadron based at Truk. Nakagawa's career had been marred by an incident before the war that meant that his promotion chances were very few and far between. On 2 February 1939, when Nakagawa was commanding the *I-60*, he had been conducting training exercises in the Bungo Straits in Japan, simulating attacks, when he had accidentally rammed the submarine *I-63* in the early morning gloom. The pressure hull breached, the *I-63* had immediately sunk, taking eighty-two of her crew with her, and Nakagawa had been placed before a court martial. He was found guilty of negligence and suspended from the navy. In 1940 he was reassigned to the command of the *I-58*, and then the *I-177*, which he took to Australian waters.

On the 26 April 1943 Nakagawa had intercepted and sunk the 8,724-ton British merchant ship *Limerick*, a member of an escorted convoy, off Cape Byron near Brisbane and escaped the resulting attack by the convoy escorts on his boat. The *Limerick* was one of five merchant ships sunk between 18 January and 29 April off the New South Wales and Queensland coasts by Japanese submarines resulting in a great loss of life among the merchant crews. Nakagawa was a man driven by a need to restore his reputation after having lost face during his court martial in 1939. Perhaps the way in which to restore his professional reputation was through achieving as many kills as possible against his country's enemies.

As the brightly lit *Centaur* crossed his path in the early hours of 14 May 1943 he did not hesitate in ordering a torpedo attack launched against her. The *Centaur* was strung with electric light bulbs that illuminated her red crosses and IRC number on the bows for all to see, but Nakagawa turned his head from the periscope eye-piece and began to issue orders for the attack plot to be drawn, and one or more torpedo tubes made ready to fire. He knew absolutely that his next actions were illegal under the rules of war, the Geneva Conventions and International Law, yet he ruthlessly ignored these facts and prepared to launch an attack. There are several ways to rationalize Nakagawa's sinking of the *Centaur*, and one is the fact that a hospital ship was tasked with collecting wounded soldiers and taking them home for treatment so that some might be returned fighting fit to once again oppose the Japanese advance. If Nakagawa sank a hospital ship he might reason that he was serving the Emperor by removing one of the links by which Australia supported her forces defending New Guinea. Perhaps what followed was revenge for Allied attacks on Japanese hospital ships? In the Allies defence, even they pointed out that the Japanese were of a habit of not properly or clearly marking their hospital ships, which led to some cases of mistaken identity. The war in the Pacific was subsequently famous for the brutality displayed by both Japanese and Allied forces towards each other, and Nakagawa may also have been aware of recent American attacks on Japanese troop transports. In January the Americans had sunk a troop transport, and thousands of the 9,500 Japanese soldiers aboard the vessel were machine gunned in the water after abandoning the sinking ship. Christopher Milligan and John Foley in *Australian Hospital Ship Centaur: The Myth of Immunity*[4] point out that in early March 1943 American aircraft had sunk an entire Japanese convoy of twenty-two ships. The majority of these vessels were troop transports, which was of course a legitimate target. However, for seven days following the initial sinking of this convoy American ships and aircraft systematically set about eliminating the survivors, machine gunning and bombing more than 3,000 of them. This action was against the established rules of war and the Geneva Conventions, which the United States had most certainly signed.

The ferocity of both combatants in the war in Asia and the Pacific was legendary, and the rule of law was very often put aside in a multitude of cases.

At 4.10 a.m. on 14 May the *Centaur* was off Moretan Island, Queensland when a Japanese torpedo struck home with deadly effect. Most of the medical staff was asleep at the moment of impact, as an enormous explosion shook the ship violently, and she caught fire and started to sink by the stern. Seaman Matthew Morris of the *Centaur*'s crew recalled those terrifying few moments as the ship foundered:

> I finished the twelve to four watch and I called the four to eight watch to go down, including me mate. And I was just havin' a cup of tea – and this big explosion, and the ship gave a shudder, and the skylight fell in on us.

In the ensuing panic Morris was able to get clear of the rapidly sinking *Centaur*:

> I don't really know how I got out of the mess room…and I'd say there was a dozen steps up to the deck. And I really can't remember going up them. But then I was washed off the back of the ship and then I realised I was in the water.[5]

Sister Ellen Savage, one of twelve members of the Australian Army Nursing Corps onboard the *Centaur*, was woken up by the torpedo slamming into the ship:

> Merle Morton and myself were awakened by two terrific explosions and practically thrown out of bed…I registered mentally that it was a torpedo explosion.

Lurching through the stricken ship onto the boat deck, the young nurses were unsure of what to do next:

> …we ran into Colonel Manson, our commanding officer, in full dress even to his cap and 'Mae West' life-jacket, who kindly said 'That's right girlies, jump for it now.' The first words I spoke was to say 'Will I have time to go back for my greatcoat?' as we were only in our pyjamas. He said 'No' and with that climbed the deck and jumped and I followed.

Savage recorded that the *Centaur* sank in only about three minutes, providing little time for the crew and passengers to abandon ship, and no time to launch any of the ship's lifeboats. Hundreds of terrified soldiers and sailors leaped into the roiling sea, and the *Centaur* disappeared taking scores of lives with her, many already dead from the torpedo impact or trapped below with no way out. The suction created by the ship plunging to the depths dragged hapless swimmers deep underwater, including Savage. She eventually surfaced in a patch of oil, suffering from an assortment of painful injuries after having been tossed and battered in the underwater whirlpool created by the *Centaur*. As Savage gasped air at the surface pain wracked her body from broken ribs, perforated eardrums and severe bruising all over. Her nose was also broken, along with her palate, but she had survived. Now came the awful realization, shared with the hundreds treading water around her, that they were far out to sea, many were injured, and there was no immediate hope of rescue.

The *I-177* was seen to surface close to the point where the *Centaur* had gone down, and many of the survivors wondered what the next Japanese move would be. The Japanese, however, made no move towards the survivors, and shortly afterwards the submarine was seen to submerge and depart from the scene, leaving the survivors to their fate.

Seaman Morris, after being washed off the stern of the *Centaur* as she sank, also found himself alone. Fortunately, Morris came upon a small, damaged life raft and clambered aboard. Later, Morris saved his friend, Seaman Teenie, by pulling him onto the raft. For many of the men and women who had managed to throw themselves clear of the *Centaur* their fates were terrible. Many could not swim and drowned after failing to find life jackets or rafts. The noises emitted by the sinking *Centaur*, as well as the thrashing of survivors in the sea and the smell of blood everywhere around the area attracted dozens of large sharks. The sharks probably scavenged floating bodies, but soon moved on to hapless swimmers and people clinging to bits of wreckage. High pitched screaming continued for hours after the sinking as people were killed by sharks and devoured. Morris and Teenie drifted on their small raft amid the horror, comforting one another, until the dawn light revealed a much more substantial raft drifting close by.

It was on this raft that Savage had managed to pull herself, along with many others, to get clear of the sharks and rest. Morris and his companion paddled over and joined the others aboard what came to be christened 'Survival Island'.

Second Officer Rippon of the *Centaur* was the senior officer to have survived the sinking and he took charge of the raft. Rippon knew that the Japanese attack had been so sudden that no distress call had been sent before the ship sank. The survivors were in dire straights unless help arrived quickly as they possessed only a little food and fresh water, and no medical supplies with which to treat the many injured lying around them. Most of the survivors were dressed in nightclothes and would suffer from exposure and hypothermia over the coming hours. Sharks constantly bumped against the raft with their snouts, or patrolled the waters all around, attacking an occasional person still in the water, or a corpse floating at the surface. Rescue was to be thirty-six hours later, and in the meantime still more of the survivors who had managed to get off the ship and onto a raft died. Morris lay next to a badly burned soldier who had ceased moving. Morris caught Savage's attention, knowing that she was a nurse, and said, 'I think this young chap's dead.' Savage leaned over and closely examined the man, confirming Morris's suspicions. Morris: '...took his identification disc off him and his name was John Walder...I gave his...disc to Sister Savage and she said: "Will you answer the Rosary?" I said: "Yes, I'll do my best." ' Private Walder was one of many buried at sea, though most likely this was more of a gesture than a possibility as bodies put over the side of the raft would have been attacked by the patrolling sharks.

Eventually Morris, Savage and the other survivors were plucked to safety by the American destroyer USS *Mugford* on 15 May, and Australia began to count the cost in lives occasioned by the loss of the *Centaur*. Of the 332 men and women on board when the ship departed from Sydney on 12 May, only sixty-seven men and one woman had been rescued by the *Mugford* four days later. It has been estimated that over 200 survived the torpedo strike and made it into the sea, but just over a quarter of those would live. Sharks, injury, drowning and despair took care of the rest, including eleven of the twelve nurses who were aboard the *Centaur*. The sinking of the *Centaur* stands as Australia's worst disaster from a submarine attack.

As for Sister Ellen Savage, the sole surviving nurse, she had spent thirty-six hours on 'Survival Island' working tirelessly to ease the suffering and pain of her companions, even though she was badly injured herself. For her courage she was awarded the George Medal. Australian Prime Minister Curtin lodged an official complaint through the neutral powers with the Japanese government over the 'barbaric' attack on an Australian hospital ship. Initially, Curtin called upon the Japanese to punish those officers responsible for the attack, but was later forced to tone down his outrage as he and other politicians feared that the Japanese might have exacted revenge on the thousands of Australian prisoners-of-war in their hands.

The man responsible for all the suffering of the people aboard the *Centaur*, Hajime Nakagawa, had actually behaved in a restrained manner considering what he was later to inflict on innocent civilians who fell into his grasp. In December 1943 Nakagawa had assumed command of submarine *I-37* (though he had still not been promoted to commander), and by February 1944 was on patrol in the Indian Ocean. On 22 February he torpedoed and sank the grain tanker *British Chivalry*. After taking the captain prisoner he ordered machine-gun fire opened up on the helpless crewmen, who were in a pair of lifeboats and lying on four rafts. Bullets rippled backwards and forwards over the defenceless survivors, the hapless captain forced to watch the massacre. Twenty sailors were killed in cold blood, and for no reason. Nakagawa struck again on 26 February, sinking the British freighter *Sutlej*, and he once again ordered his crew to machine-gun the survivors. On 29 February the *I-37* sank the British merchant ship *Ascot*, and the crew had taken to lifeboats, life rafts or were swimming in the sea. The Japanese skipper first ordered his submarine to deliberately ram the *Ascot*'s lifeboats, killing some of the survivors and tipping the rest into the ocean. Machine guns were turned once more upon the fifty-two men struggling in the sea, other Japanese took pot-shots at their bobbing heads with pistols, some were even dragged aboard the deck and carved up with swords and a few finished off by being pounded to death with sledge hammers before their bodies were dumped back into the sea. Forty-four men were killed in this manner before the Japanese slunk away.

Judged in the light of these appalling later crimes, it is intriguing as to why Nakagawa did not let loose his evident bloodlust upon the survivors of the *Centaur* eight months before. Combined Fleet Headquarters had issued an order to submarine skippers on 20 March 1943 which stated: 'Do not stop with the sinking of enemy ships and cargoes; at the same time that you carry out the complete destruction of the crews of enemy ships, if possible, seize part of the crew and endeavour to secure information about the enemy.' The application of this chilling order appears to have been left to the discretion of individual commanders. Nakagawa, when placed on trial in 1949 for the various outrages he had ordered committed, used the 'I was only following orders' plea to attempt to deflect his guilt. Sadly, much of the evidence entered in the trial was disallowed, and this meant that Nakagawa was classed as a Category B war criminal and only received eight years hard labour. In 1954, after only six years, the mass murderer submariner was released, and continued to deny that he had ever sunk the *Centaur* up until his death. Indeed, the Japanese government only officially acknowledged that the *I-177* had sunk the *Centaur* in 1979.

After sinking the *Centaur* Nakagawa took the *I-177* back to Truk and made a second war patrol to the Australian east coast in June, but went to Rabaul in July after making no further attacks on Allied ships.

On 29 April the *I-180* found the small Norwegian freighter *Fingal* that was on her way from Sydney to Port Darwin under Australian government contract, transporting ammunition to Coffs Harbour, New South Wales. The *Fingal* was not such an inviting opportunity as she was under escort by the powerful American destroyer escort USS *Patterson*. Kusaka pressed home his attack regardless of the risk and managed to place a torpedo portside aft, with another smashing into the engine room tearing the guts out of the 2,137-ton ship. The Norwegian sank in less than one minute, taking several of her crew with her. The *Patterson* eventually rescued nineteen out of the crew of thirty-one.

The *I-180* continued to lurk around Coffs Harbour into May, and Kusaka's patience was rewarded with another good target that presented itself on the 12th. Convoy PG50, consisting of fifteen ships, was sailing from Cairns to Sydney. Kusaka fired a spread of torpedoes, and would have been more successful if not for torpedo malfunction. One torpedo detonated inside the 5,832-ton American freighter *Ormiston*, loaded with bagged sugar, blowing a hole in her portside. A second torpedo struck the Australian ship *Caradale*, but the contact exploder fitted to the warhead failed to detonate and the torpedo did nothing more than leave a dent in the freighter's hull before sinking to the seabed. Two Australian and an American warship took the *Ormiston* in tow, and after temporary repairs were effected in Coffs Harbour the freighter continued on her way to Sydney. By the end of May Kusaka and the *I-180* were back in Truk after a disappointing patrol.

Meanwhile, the *I-178* returned to Australia for a second war patrol, and on 17 June while the submarine was sixty-five miles south-east of Coffs Harbour, a Beaufort of 32 Squadron, RAAF, pounced on her. A second Beaufort joined in the attack on the surfaced submarine, inflicting some damage. The aircraft left the scene after reporting that the submarine was trailing a large oil slick in her wake, and the *I-178* was never heard from again. It was a notable kill for the Australians, eighty-nine Japanese losing their lives.

Formerly the *I-74*, the re-numbered *I-174* under the command of Lieutenant Nobukiyo Nambu departed Truk on 16 May 1943 with orders to patrol off the east coast of Australia. In her earlier incarnation as the *I-74* she had participated in the Pearl Harbor operation, as well as assisting with the flying boat raid on Pearl Harbor in May 1942, all under her then skipper, Lieutenant-Commander Kusaka. Nambu assumed command of the boat on 12 November 1942, as Kusaka had left to assist with the working-up of the *I-180* and was later to command the giant *I-400*. On 27 May 1943 Nambu and the *I-174* appeared off the Australian coast at Sandy Cape and began patrolling for targets along the coast. The next day the submarine was spotted on radar by a Bristol Beaufort of 32 Squadron, RAAF, which was on anti-submarine patrol from Bundaberg. Sharp-eyed lookouts on the Japanese boat spied the Beaufort as it attempted to creep up on the submarine and Nambu was able to crash-dive and escape.

On 1 June the *I-174* was seventy miles east of Brisbane, hoping for an encounter with an enemy ship. Sailing towards the Japanese hunter was a lone merchant ship, and Nambu immediately began manoeuvring his submarine into an attack position. The vessel was a 3,303-ton American freighter, *Point San Pedro*, sailing towards Brisbane from the Panama Canal. When the merchant captain sighted the submarine he immediately began zigzagging in a desperate attempt to throw off the Japanese officers' aim, but four torpedoes were nonetheless launched at the ship. By sheer good luck, and perhaps because of the ship's erratic movements, all four torpedoes completely missed, and the radio operator was instructed to inform the Australian authorities of a Japanese submarine lurking close to Brisbane. The Australians reacted with the dispatch of an Avro Anson maritime bomber of 71 Squadron, RAAF, with orders to seek out and destroy the boat. A further six Anson's left the airfields at Lowood and Coffs Harbour to join in the search but found no trace of the *I-174*.

Nambu was a submarine skipper of some temerity and, some might say, suicidal impulses. On the afternoon of 3 June he sighted a small convoy of six freighters being escorted by three destroyers off Brisbane, and he decided to attempt an attack. Coming to the surface at 6 p.m., he ordered his diesel engines full ahead, and grinding hastily through the waves Nambu began to pursue the convoy. Not surprisingly his submarine was soon spotted by lookouts on the various ships, and the destroyers swung around and began to close the distance between the convoy and the *I-174*. The Japanese submarine crash-dived and fled from the scene before the convoy escorts could plaster the boat with depth charges and Hedgehog mortar bombs.

The next day Nambu attempted to intercept another lone ship, this time a US Army transport named the *Edward Chambers*, another ship on her way from the Panama Canal to Brisbane loaded with supplies. Nambu spotted the 4,113-ton merchant-man at 8.45 a.m. off Cape Moreton while his submarine was submerged, and he made belaboured efforts to close the distance between the two vessels in order to launch his torpedoes. Deciding instead to blow the *Edward Chambers* out of the water with his deck-gun Nambu ordered the *I-174* to the surface. At 9.48 a.m. the gunners unmasked their fire, nine shells sailing past

171

the merchant ship without achieving a single hit. In fact, the army gunners aboard the *Edward Chambers* returned fire using a 3-inch gun mounted on the stern, and twelve American shells splashed into the sea close to the submarine, which caused Nambu to break off his attack and submerge. By now large numbers of Australian aircraft had been sent aloft to search out the errant submarine, and the *I-174* remained submerged for the rest of the day fearing aerial attack.

At 10.25 a.m. on 5 June the *I-174* was still submerged sixty miles north-east of Coffs Harbour, the hydrophone operator listening for enemy activity. What was clearly discerned were the propeller sounds of several ships that were apparently moving in a convoy several miles from the submarine. Nambu moved the *I-174* behind convoy PG53, and surfaced in poor weather. The weather was bad enough to have concealed the approach of Nambu's boat, but he decided to take no chances so when a shadowing patrol aircraft came close he submerged and waited for it to move off before he resumed closing in on the convoy's tail. The pursuit took Nambu all day, and by the time the sun was beginning to fade on the horizon he had managed to bring his vessel to within 6,000 yards of the convoy without being spotted. Creeping ever closer Nambu prepared to fire but an escorting destroyer spotted the shadowing Japanese submarine and turned hard about and charged. His approach ruined, Nambu had no choice but to crash-dive once more. No depth charges followed the submarine's descent, and at 9.45 p.m. Nambu brought the *I-174* back to the surface for another try at the convoy. Another charge by a destroyer forced him back beneath the waves, but Nambu had already noted the convoy's course and speed and he decided that instead of constantly popping up behind the ships, and attracting the unwanted attentions of the escorts, he would instead pile on the speed and attempt to place his submarine in a position by first light ahead of the convoy. Running his diesels at the surface Nambu brought the *I-174* to the position where he estimated the convoy would eventually appear and then settled down at periscope depth to wait.[6]

On the morning of 6 June the *I-174* ascended to the surface, but Nambu's careful planning had placed him at too great a range to intercept the convoy passing in front of him in the distance without risking being caught by patrolling Australian aircraft as he tried to close the gap. Undoubtedly disappointed he abandoned stalking convoy PG53 and instead motored off towards the south, heading for the waters around Newcastle and Sydney that he hoped would be teeming with ships.

The next day the *I-174* was 100 miles east of Sydney. Lookouts spotted a single ship at 4.50 a.m., and Nambu began once more to plan his approach and attack. The ship was the *John Bartram*, a 7,176-ton American Liberty approaching Sydney after crossing the Pacific from San Francisco. As the submarine charged down the distance between the two vessels the American captain began zigzagging to stall the inevitable torpedo attack that was to follow. Nambu managed to get the *I-174* ahead of his target and launched a spread of four torpedoes at 6.06 a.m. In a confused attack two of the torpedoes definitely missed the ship, and another exploded prematurely, rocking the *I-174*. Perhaps wanting to finally record a kill, Nambu erroneously believed that he had struck the *John Bartram*. The *I-174* departed the scene in some haste, its commander satisfied that he had sunk his target. The *John Bartram* sailed on undamaged.

Nambu next spent several days hanging around the approaches to Sydney without sighting a single ship, which was unusual considering the density of merchant and warship traffic travelling in and out of the port. At 2 p.m. on 13 June Nambu finally sighted a small convoy of approximately six transport ships, escorted by a pair of destroyers, about thirty miles east of the Wollongong Lighthouse. Once again, the *I-174* surfaced too far from the ships to allow an interception to be attempted and Nambu was forced to submerge again and wait. The next night, another Beaufort on anti-submarine duty pounced on the *I-174*, and the submarine narrowly avoided a hail of bombs. After staying submerged for over half an hour Nambu resurfaced only to discover that the Australian aircraft was still circling the area and he was attacked again and forced once more beneath the waves.

On 16 June, when the *I-174* was south-east of Coffs Harbour, Nambu finally discovered a convoy that he was in a position to attack. Five corvettes screened the convoy, including HMAS *Deloraine*, but the *I-174* slipped past the warships and, at 5.20 p.m., fired two torpedoes at a pair of transports. The first torpedo struck the 5,000-ton Landing Ship Tank, *LST 469* in the starboard side, towards the stern. The detonation completely destroyed the vessel's steering gear and also killed twenty-six men, but *LST-469* remained afloat. A few moments later the second torpedo struck the starboard side of the 5,551-ton US Army transport ship *Portmar*. The detonation of the Japanese torpedo set a massive fire in the *Portmar*'s holds, which in turn set off ammunition stored aboard the ship. The crew soon abandoned the stricken ship, and after only seven minutes the *Portmar* sank. Two of the escorting corvettes ineffectually depth-charged the *I-174*. Lieutenant Nambu goes down in history as the last Japanese submarine skipper to successfully sink a ship off the east coast of Australia, and on 20 June the *I-174* was ordered back to Trùk. Nambu was later reassigned as commander of the submarine aircraft carrier *I-401*, and American aircraft east of Truk destroyed his former command, the *I-174*, on 12 April 1944.[7]

Notes
1. Data derived from Bob Hackett & Sander Kingsepp's http://www.combined-fleet.com/I-21.htm
2. ibid.
3. *The Sinking of the Centaur*, Commonwealth Department of Veterans' Affairs, http://www.dva.gov.au
4. Christopher S. Milligan & John C.H. Foley, *Australian Hospital Ship Centaur: The Myth of Immunity*, (Hendra: Nairana Publications), 1993
5. *The Sinking of the Centaur*, Commonwealth Department of Veterans' Affairs, http://www.dva.gov.au
6. Partly derived from Bob Hackett & Sander Kingsepp's http://www.com-binedfleet.com/I-174.htm
7. ibid.

Chapter 9

Storm From a Clear Sky

*There is nothing more dreadful than crazy persons. The Japanese
are a crazy nation in fighting...the Japanese are always ready to
throw away their lives for a nation; they regard their lives as
lightly as they do the weather.*

Count Okuma, a Japanese aristocrat writing in 1906

The final occasion on which a Japanese submarine operated close
to the west coast of the United States was in October 1944, after
an absence by Japanese forces from American coastal waters of
over two years. Following the Battle of Leyte Gulf the *I-12*, under
Commander Kameo Kudo, set out from Japan on 4 October with
orders to attack enemy commerce between the Hawaiian Islands
and San Francisco.

Completed at Kawasaki's Kobe yard in May 1944, the 2,943-
ton *I-12* was a Type-A2 submarine, and the only one of her class.
The type was identical in all regards to the Type-A1, one of
which, the *I-9*, had acted as a command vessel coordinating
Japanese submarine activities off the American west coast in early
1942. The only difference between the *I-12* and the earlier models
was a decrease in power, and an extended operational range of
22,000 nautical miles at 16 knots. This made the submarine ideal
for operations off the American coast.

In October 1944 the *I-12* was reassigned directly to 6th Fleet
and given the unenviable task of returning a Japanese submarine
presence to the waters off the United States. Commander Kudo
was instructed to take the *I-12* from Japan directly to the waters
off California and to attack merchant ship convoys. After a run
along the west coast Kudo was to backtrack to Hawaii, then sail

175

to Tahiti and finally to a point east of the Marshall Islands before returning home. The Japanese could spare only a single submarine for the operation at this stage of the war as the strategic situation inexorably deteriorated for Japan. This was in contrast to the nine Japanese submarines that had deployed along the west coast during early 1942.

On 4 October the *I-12* left Kure and motored towards its fate. On 30 October Kudo came upon a lone ship in the North Pacific steaming from San Francisco to Honolulu, and he attacked immediately. The ship was the *John A. Johnson*, a 7,176-ton American Liberty ship loaded down with 7,000 tons of supplies, including army trucks lined up on her decks, bound for the troops fighting in the Pacific. She carried a crew of forty-one, plus twenty-eight US Navy armed guards to man her several self-defence guns and a single army officer who was in charge of the cargo. The *John A. Johnson* was sailing at a ponderous 9 knots, with all lights extinguished and she was maintaining a strict radio silence. At 9.10 p.m. the first torpedo struck her starboard side, tearing loose the trucks stored on deck, and knocking the gunners and crewmen off their feet. Even though dealt a crippling blow, the armed guards, unaware of how badly damaged their ship was, raced to return fire at the unseen Japanese submarine. According to the account of one of their number, Seaman Harold L. Clark:

Lieutenant Yates came up and told me to help man the number 6 gun. I proceeded to the number 6 gun, and there sighted [the] explosion just astern of [the] ship. It looked like another torpedo. The ship began to break in two.[1]

The crew hastily abandoned the foundering vessel, and took to the lifeboats and rafts:

We saw [an] object about three hundred feet away from us. We signaled object thinking it was another raft and it returned the signal. It came to the surface and turned out to be the submarine, and it started coming toward us.[2]

The *John A. Johnson*'s back had been broken by the torpedo detonations, and as the crew watched from their lifeboats and rafts the ship broke into two sections that stayed afloat. Kudo had dark plans for the men marooned in their little boats far out at sea. When the *I-12* broke the surface the main deck-gun was immediately manned and made ready. In the meantime machine guns had been brought up from below onto the *I-12*'s conning tower bridge. Surging forwards, the bow of the *I-12* slammed into one of the lifeboats, tumbling terrified survivors into the sea, and at the same moment a clatter of machine-gun fire poured forth from the conning tower. Japanese seamen sprayed a murderous and indiscriminate fire onto the helpless men in the lifeboats or swimming in the water, Japanese officers also taking pot shots at the sailors with their pistols. Aboard Clark's raft they fearfully watched the approaching submarine:

> About one hundred and fifty feet from us, [the] submarine machine-gunned us. I could see tracers going over our heads. We jumped into [the] water. Submarine passed by about one hundred and fifty feet. We swam back and got on the raft. Submarine circled and came back at us again.[3]

Men desperately attempted to row their lifeboats clear of the pirate submarine and its murderous crew. The *I-12* surged through the mass of lifeboats and rafts and kept firing, 'We dove into the water again,' recalled Clark, as the Japanese renewed their attention on his raft. 'This time [the] submarine hit the raft, and as it passed by they fired again with [a] machine gun, tracers hitting [the] water near me.'[4] The *I-12* came close enough to the men in the water for Clark to notice: 'Five American flags were painted on the port side of the bow. Men on the submarine were yelling "Bonzi" [sic] and cursing at us.'[5] About half an hour after they had attempted to murder the crew, Japanese gunners fired a fusillade of shells at the two sections of the former *John A. Johnson* until they caught fire, exploded and sometime around dawn the following day sank. Six merchant seamen were killed and many wounded, before darkness finally ended the Japanese attack and the *I-12* submerged and made off from the scene of the crime. It was the flames and explosions resulting from the Japanese assault on the two sections of the *John A. Johnson* that assisted in the men's rescue from the ocean. A Pan American Airways airliner spotted the flames far below and managed to signal to the lifeboats, and the pilot reported what he had seen to the US Navy in San Francisco. The USS *Argus* rescued the men at noon the day after the attack.

The *I-12* would earn her comeuppance for the sadistic murder of innocent sailors, and retribution was not long in coming. Sailing away from the west coast, Kudo headed into the mid-Pacific and reported to 6th Fleet headquarters during late December that he had managed to sink an enemy tanker and another freighter, though this claim has never been confirmed. The last anyone ever heard of Commander Kudo and the 113 other officers and men aboard the *I-12* was a radio transmission sent on 15 January 1945. Kudo reported that enemy forces north of the Marshall Islands had located his submarine. No one knows what fate befell the *I-12*, and the Japanese noted on 31 January that the vessel had been lost with all hands sometime after the receipt of that final radio message.

Japan's submarine construction programme eventually produced the single most extraordinary class of boats conceived by any of the combatant navies of the Second World War. The I-400-class submarines were created in order to take Fujita's original plan to attack the United States on home ground to a devastating conclusion. Fujita's plan was dusted off, read again and evaluated, and the problems of the September 1942 missions over the forests of Oregon analysed. Solutions were sought to make any future attacks a success.

As early as April 1942 the Imperial Navy had decided to order the construction of a class of submarine that would dwarf previous Japanese creations in order to provide a far-reaching strike capacity. The problems with Fujita's original concept were obvious and based around the equipment the Japanese had utilized when making the attacks. The Yokosuka E14Y1 float-plane was not a dedicated bomber, but a reconnaissance plane that could be used as a bomber, capable of carrying a tiny munitions payload. The bomb load was pathetically small, and getting the aircraft in range of a ground target was largely a waste of naval resources. The aircraft was also ponderously slow, with a cruising speed of only 90 miles per hour, which although making it an ideal reconnaissance platform, also made it very vulnerable to anti-aircraft fire and enemy fighters. The E14Y1 was also virtually defenceless, armed with a single rear firing 7.7mm machine gun, so if it had encountered an enemy fighter it would in all probability have been shot down with ease. The submarines that were fitted with the E14Y1, such as the *I-25*, were only able to store a single aircraft inside their waterproof hangar. The only conceivable way the Japanese could have mounted a sizeable raid with these little planes would have been by gathering several submarines together off the American coast, which in itself was a waste of the submarines' own fighting potential as they waited around for the return of their aircraft, and exposed the boats to the risk of aerial and ship attacks.

The answer to all of these problems was a single submarine large enough to both reach land targets in the United States without requiring any refuelling, and able to carry more than one aircraft. The new bombers would have to be potent weapons, able to deliver a large payload of bombs, but still retaining the floatplane characteristics enabling their operation at sea from submarines. In effect, the Japanese Navy required a submarine aircraft carrier, and this is exactly what they set about designing and constructing between April 1942 and December 1944.

Each I-400-class vessel was a monster, the largest submarines built until well into the post-war nuclear age, their size only surpassed in 1962 when the Americans commissioned the USS *Lafayette*. Displacing 5,223-tons surfaced, each boat was 400.3 feet in length with a beam of 39.3 feet and was powered by four diesel engines and electric motors. Atop the weather deck was a 115 feet long waterproof hanger, twelve feet wide, big enough for three specially designed torpedo bombers. In front of the hangar, bolted to the immense deck stretched a pneumatic aircraft-launching catapult eighty-five feet long, and alongside this a powerful hydraulic crane for recovering the aircraft from the sea.[6] Through the Yanagi underwater trade in weapons and new technologies conducted between Nazi Germany and the Japanese, the Imperial Navy had copied the snorkel technology fitted to late-war U-boats, and these were fitted to all four I-400-class submarines. The snorkel mast, when extended above the surface of the water as the submarine cruised at periscope depth, enabled the boat to run on its diesel engines instead of batteries, producing a greatly increased underwater speed and protection from aerial detection and attack. Hugely capacious fuel tanks on each boat meant that each of these submarine aircraft carriers was capable of cruising an astounding 35,500 nautical miles at 14 knots before the tanks ran dry, in other words giving the Japanese skipper the ability to circumnavigate the globe one and a half times. The huge range of these vessels meant that for the first time in the war the Japanese Navy had a machine capable of not only crossing the Pacific to attack the west coast of the United States, but also, in theory, of crossing into the Atlantic via Cape Horn and unleashing air strikes against New York or Washington DC, and both cities were later seriously considered by naval planners in Tokyo for attacks. The I-400-class submarines were capable of a top surface or submerged snorkel speed of 18.7 knots, or if fully submerged and running on electric motors 6.5 knots. Radar and radar detectors, though not up to the German standard, were fitted to all four boats of the class. Although submarine aircraft carriers the I-400-class boats were more than capable of fighting like any other submarine types, having eight torpedo tubes (and twenty torpedoes) and an improved 140mm 50 calibre deck-gun. Improved anti-aircraft defences increased each boat's chances of standing off an aerial assault, with a 25mm cannon mounted on the conning tower, and three triple barrelled 25mm cannon located on top of the aircraft hangar, giving a total of ten guns. With a maximum diving depth of almost 330 feet, each boat took slightly under one minute to crash-dive.[7]

Such superb and powerful vessels required an equally superb and capable aircraft type, and here the Japanese also excelled. Each I-400-class submarine was designed to carry a maximum of three Aichi M6A1 Seiran torpedo bombers. Seiran can be translated as 'Storm from the sky',[8] and these aircraft were no ponderous reconnaissance types but sturdy birds of destruction. Still floatplanes, each monoplane measured thirty-five feet in length, with a wingspan of forty feet. Designed by Toshio Ozaki, chief engineer at Aichi, the Seiran had to conform to a series of guidelines laid down by the Imperial Navy as they sought the perfect plane for their new submarines. In late 1942 Ozaki began developing the aircraft that the navy specified must have been capable of carrying a maximum bomb load consisting of a single

1,288-lb (800kg) aerial bomb or torpedo. In the light of the desperate position Japan was in by late 1944, if a kamikaze mission was called for the floats could be detached and the fuel and bomb load increased for a one-way mission against the enemy. The navy also stipulated that the aircraft must be capable of a top speed of 294 miles per hour with floats, or 347 miles per hour with the floats detached. Under normal, non-kamikaze, operating conditions each Seiran had a range of 654 miles, which meant that the 'mother' submarine could sit some way off from the enemy shore when launching and recovering its air group, instead of having to come close inshore to launch and then sit vulnerably on the surface awaiting an aircraft's return from its sortie.

The first prototype Seiran was completed in October 1943, and several others followed. The navy, however, was overjoyed with the performance of the prototype aircraft and ordered full production before testing had been completed at Aichi in early 1944. This decision was probably hastened by the deteriorating Japanese naval situation, and the necessity of getting the new submarines and aircraft into action as soon as possible. This was to prove to be no easy task as American bombing raids and even an earthquake, which completely shut down production at Aichi by March 1945, hampered production of the aircraft. In the end Aichi engineers managed to cobble together twenty-six Seiran torpedo bombers (including prototypes) and a pair of land-based trainers, the M6A1-K Nanzan. The navy no longer required a large number of Seiran aircraft as they had been forced by the weakening of Japan's economy to scale back the number of I-400 -class submarines under construction. The *I-400* was ready for service on 30 December 1944, and the *I-401* followed a few days later. *I-402*'s duties were changed from being an underwater aircraft carrier, and instead she was refitted as a submarine fuel tanker. Two other boats, *I-404* and *I-405* were abandoned on the slips and not completed before the Japanese surrender.

Although each I-400-class submarine's complement was listed officially as 145 men, on operations up to 220 crewmen were carried aboard in order to make the dispatching and recovering of the aircraft as efficient an operation as possible. The Seiran aircraft were stored inside the huge hangar with their floats detached, and their wings and tails folded up. Each well-trained team of aircraft technicians and mechanics could assemble a single aircraft in around seven minutes, ready for launching. All three torpedo bombers could be assembled, fuelled and fitted with either torpedoes or aerial bombs, attached to the launching ramp and catapulted away in about forty-five minutes (close enough to the original Japanese Navy stipulation of thirty minutes). In order to maintain the air group while the submarine was at sea a special compartment was located inside the pressure hull beneath the hangar where engineers could test aircraft engines and maintain the airframes. Beside this was the aircraft magazine, containing four aerial torpedoes, fifteen bombs and ammunition for the aircraft's cannon and machine guns.[9]

The *I-400* and *I-401* were placed into a new unit alongside two modified AM-class submarines, the *I-13* and *I-14*. Originally this type of boat had only been capable of carrying a single floatplane, but while under construction in 1944 the Japanese changed their plans and altered the configuration of the AM-class boats to take two of the new Seiran bombers. Although having a range of 21,000 nautical miles at 16 knots, the modifications meant the boats' underwater performance suffered, making them relatively easy targets for both American aircraft and warships.[10] Under the overall command of Captain Tatsunosuke Ariizumi, the submarines were organized as 1st Submarine Flotilla, with the aircraft and aircrew forming the new 631st Air Corps. The *I-13* and *I-14* would each carry two aircraft, while the I-400-class pair was loaded with full air groups of three Seiran each. The Japanese Navy now had the most potent collection of submarines yet assembled in war, and what was required now was a plan to use all of this potential against the enemy.

The Japanese Army had for years been experimenting with biological warfare at a secret research facility at Harbin in China. In 1936 the army had organized Unit 731 under Colonel Dr Shiro Ishii. The experiments had been conducted on human beings, both Chinese soldiers and civilians and American prisoners captured in the Philippines in 1942, and the results had demonstrated that various lethal bacteria and diseases could be used against civilian populaces, and delivered either by dropping infected insects or rats or delivering the bacteria in special aerial bombs. Tens of thousands died as a result of infected fleas being dropped over wide areas of the Chinese countryside. The Japanese also managed to kill around 1,700 of their own troops when the experiments backfired. At this stage of the war, with Japan clearly losing, some in the navy advocated using the ten aircraft of 1st Submarine Flotilla to drop bubonic plague, cholera, dengue fever, typhus, anthrax or a wide variety of other virulent bacterial agents on the United States in order to create widespread infection and panic among their enemies. A leading advocate of such a strategy was Vice-Admiral Jisaburo Ozawa, then Vice-Chief of the Naval General Staff in Tokyo, who along with others formulated a plan codenamed Operation 'PX' to this end. This plan envisaged the dropping of infected fleas into the downtown area of San Francisco from Seiran aircraft, an event that would have killed thousands of Americans. However, there were those in positions of higher command who considered such a plan to be lunacy, and stated this quite emphatically at the time. A leading member of the opposition to 'PX' was the army's most senior officer, General Yoshijiro Umezu. Umezu was Chief of the General Staff, and managed to quash the plan on 26 March 1945 before any move was made to carry it out.

This diabolical operation was a massive step on from Fujita's modest bombing proposals, and even for many Japanese dropping plagues into the enemy camp was going too far. As for Unit 731, when the war ended Ishii and his group of scientists and soldiers were captured by the Americans. Instead of hauling these mass murderers before a war crimes tribunal the Americans struck a deal whereby the members of Unit 731 were granted immunity from prosecution in return for passing their germ warfare data to the Americans. The exigencies of the new Cold War with the Soviet Union meant that the United States was prepared to overlook how this data had been created in order to stay one step ahead of its enemy.

Although Operation 'PX' was dropped, the Imperial Navy still wanted to launch its ten Seiran aircraft against targets in America, but this time armed with conventional weapons. Various targets were placed before the naval staff, including San Francisco, New York and Washington DC, as well as the Panama Canal, ironically once Fujita's target of choice. All things being considered, the navy eventually decided that a strike against the Panama Canal would have had the greatest effect on America's ability to prosecute the war against Japan. The specific target that the Japanese identified as creating the most damage would have been a strike aimed at destroying the Gatun Locks. The Panama Canal is very different from its much longer cousin, the Suez Canal. The Suez Canal remains at sea level for its entire length, whereas the Panama Canal has six sets of locks to raise and lower ships along its course. Water for these locks comes from two artificial lakes, Gatun and Madden. If the lock gates could be breached Gatun Lake would empty itself, making the canal impassable for American shipping for several months and severely disrupting the American build-up in the Pacific. It was reasoned that the ten Seiran torpedo bombers would be able to breach the locks in a determined attack, and it would be the last place the Americans would expect a sudden Japanese aerial assault, so surprise might also have meant encountering little opposition at the target. It was planned that the ten Seirans would attack the Gatun Locks with six aerial torpedoes and four conventional bombs. The trip from Japan to Panama and back again would be 17,000 nautical miles, and the Japanese would require 6,400-tons of diesel fuel for the four submarines. This quantity was not available at the submarine base at Kure in Japan. Therefore, before the plan could be launched an annoying delay ensued as the *I-401* was sent to Darien in China to obtain the necessary fuel and transport it back to Japan.

The *I-401*'s cruise across to Manchuria would take her through the Inland Sea, where the voyage almost ended in disaster. American B-29 Superfortress bombers, as well as flattening Japanese cities in fire raids, had also been busily mining areas of the Inland Sea known to still be used by the remaining surface and submarine forces of the shattered Japanese Navy. The Americans were also, by this stage of the war, able to operate aircraft carriers off the Japanese coast with virtual impunity. On 19 March 1945 Vice-Admiral Marc Mitscher led his Task Force 58[11] on a devastating attack on the Kure Naval Arsenal. Over 240 American carrier planes bombed and strafed the remains of the once great Imperial Navy. As well as the huge I-400-class submarines drawn up in dry-docks, the *I-13* was in the harbour and narrowly escaped damage. The Japanese battleships *Yamato, Haruna,*

Hyuga and *Ise* were all bombed and strafed, as well as Japan's remaining aircraft carriers *Kaiyo, Amagi, Ryuho* and *Katsuragi*.

It was onto an American aerial mine that the *I-401* bumped on 12 April off Hime Shima Lighthouse in the Inland Sea, and although the damage she sustained was not terminal, the vessel had to head back to Kure for repairs. In her stead the *I-400* was sent across to Darien and managed to secure the necessary fuel and transport it safely back to Japan. With the acquisition of the fuel, and the return to service of the *I-401* following hasty repairs, the stage looked set for the attack on the Panama Canal. The Japanese now decided to carefully train for the proposed operation, constructing a life-size replica of the Gatun Lock gates in Toyama Bay so that the Seiran pilots could make dummy attack runs. The training period was fraught with dangers for the submarines and aircraft as the Americans had, by this stage, almost complete mastery of the air over the Home Islands and American submarines lurked close inshore sinking any remaining merchant ships with impunity. Mines dropped by B-29s littered the sea routes, and the *I-401*'s recent collision with one demonstrated how vulnerable Japanese submarines had become, a situation being faced at the same time by German U-boats attempting to train crews and work up their new Type XXI and XXIII electro-boats in Baltic waters, heavily mined by the RAF. Captain Ariizumi watched his squadron preparing for the forthcoming attack and he grew increasingly confident that the strike would be a success as the pilots laboured to accurately hit the mocked-up lock gates time and time again.

However bold and far-reaching a strike the Panama Canal raid would have been, it was events closer to home that diverted the Japanese High Command's attention, and made them change the focus of the 1st Submarine Flotilla attack. Panama was a long way away in the minds of many Japanese strategists, who examined their maps with growing anxiety as they watched thousands of American and British ships congregating close to the Home Islands in preparation for the projected invasion of Japan itself. Perhaps the new submarine aircraft carriers would be better employed in attacking the enemy ship concentrations closer to Japan than crossing the Pacific to points distant? Ariizumi was astounded when he was informed that he was to abandon further training for a strike against the Panama Canal, just at the point when he believed his submarines and aircraft were ready to commence the operation, and he was directed instead to take his squadron out against the American anchorage at Ulithi Atoll. The message Ariizumi received from headquarters read: 'A man does not worry about a fire he sees on the horizon when other flames are licking at his kimono!' but this did little to placate the squadron commander's anger and protestations over the change in plan. Headquarters refused to change its mind, and ordered Ariizumi to conduct an air strike against Ulithi in mid-August, necessitating a completely new plan and little time to prepare the boats or the aircrew. This was Operation Hikari, an operation that envisaged six Seirans of 631st Air Corps launching a concerted kamikaze attack on the American anchorage.

The *I-13* was the first of the new submarines to proceed with the changed operation, moving to Ominato Naval Base on Honshu Island on 4 July. There she was loaded with two crated Nakajima C6N2 Ayagumo reconnaissance aircraft, the planes destined to assist the 631st Air Group pilots with finding targets at Ulithi. Once loaded aboard Commander Ohashi headed directly for the Japanese base at Truk. On 14 July the *I-14* took the same route to Truk in preparation for the attack scheduled to commence on 17 August 1945.

The *I-13* never made it to her destination, as she was intercepted 550 miles east of Yokosuka on the early morning of 16 July by aircraft from the carrier USS *Anzio*. A Grumman Avenger discovered the submarine on the surface and immediately engaged it with machine-gun fire and 5-inch rockets. The damaged *I-13* crash-dived, and the Avenger pilot dropped a Fido homing torpedo in her wake, as well as several depth charges. A further two Avengers arrived at the scene and dropped another homing torpedo into the sea. Later that morning the destroyer USS *Lawrence C. Taylor* finished off the damaged submarine with a pattern of twenty-four 7.2-inch Hedgehog mortar bombs, killing all 140 Japanese aboard the vessel.[12]

Commander Toshio Kusaka aboard the *I-400* cruised confidently out of Ominato harbour on 23 July, followed soon after by Lieutenant-Commander Shinsei Nambu and the *I-401*. Both vessels were travelling on different routes for safety, but planned to rendezvous three weeks hence south-east of Ulithi. The *I-14* arrived at Truk on 4 August and unloaded two crated Ayagumo reconnaissance aircraft. The waters around Ulithi were soon to be infested with Japanese submarines carrying Kaiten human torpedoes, excluding the submarine aircraft carriers, as the Imperial Navy bet everything it had on smashing the American fleet anchorage with suicide attacks.

The Japanese had modified a torpedo as a suicide weapon and aptly christened it Kaiten (returning to the heavens). Only the Type-1 one-man model fitted with a 3,000-pound warhead was used on operations, the Japanese deploying about 100 in the dying months of the war. It was not a very effective weapon as Allied warships and aircraft easily sank them. The Kaiten only managed to sink two American ships, the USS *Mississenewa* on 20 November 1944 and the USS *Underhill* on 24 July 1945. However, the Japanese continued to deploy the Kaiten until the end of the war, a large submarine carrying up to six that could be launched while the boat was submerged.

Unfortunately for the Japanese, their huge new I-400-class submarines, and the planes they carried, were in the end destined never to see action. The attack on Ulithi Atoll had been scheduled for 17 August, but as the submarines made their way into position the Japanese government capitulated following the atomic bombings of Hiroshima and Nagasaki and surrendered unconditionally on 15 August. For Captain Ariizumi the news of Japan's defeat just as his well-trained and committed squadron was about to demonstrate their worth to the navy and the nation was shattering. The Emperor himself had addressed the nation and its armed forces and ordered them all to cease fighting, and none of the submarine captains would go against his word. Naval headquarters in Tokyo ordered all submarines to raise a black flag and return to their home ports on the surface. All that was left for Ariizumi was to empty his vessels of anything the hated Americans might like to examine when they came to take possession of his boats. All sensitive documents, code-books and signalling equipment was pitched over the side, along with ammunition for the submarines' weapons. In a few hours of mad activity Japanese submariners set about firing off all their torpedoes, and onboard the *I-401* the crew catapulted pilotless

Seiran bombers off the vessels into the sea. On the *I-400* the Japanese sailors punched great holes in the three Seirans floats and then pushed the aircraft overboard. On 28 August, as the three I-400-class submarines closed on Japan they were overtaken by American forces, their colours were struck, and duly replaced with the Stars and Stripes. Taken over by the US Navy, both the *I-400* and the *I-401* were sailed across the Pacific, ironically to the American west coast they had been designed and built to strike. There the boats were extensively tested, and along with surrendered German U-boats the technologies of their former enemies were integrated into submarine designs for the Cold War. After they had outlived their usefulness the Americans towed the vessels out into the Pacific and scuttled them in 1946. The *I-402*, the only other completed I-400-class submarine, never undertook a mission to transport fuel to Japan and was also scuttled by the Americans in 1946. When work ceased on the *I-404* and *I-405*, the former submarine was ninety per cent complete. Both vessels were later scrapped where they lay. The only survivor of the I-400-class project is a single Seiran torpedo bomber, discovered by the Americans in the ruins of the Aichi factory in 1945, taken back to the United States for testing and display, and now, after a complete rebuild, displayed at the National Air and Space Museum in Washington DC. In a final footnote to the story, in March 2005 a deep diving submersible from the Hawaii Undersea Research Laboratory located the wreck of the *I-401* off Oahu.

In the end Fujita's plan of 1942, to strike against the American mainland, has been recorded in the history books as a mere two feeble aircraft sorties over the great forests of Oregon. The planned Japanese operation for 1945, striking the Gatun Locks at the Panama Canal as Fujita had suggested years before, never went ahead because the Japanese decided to confront the enemy closer to home. Fortunately for everyone concerned, the evil Operation 'PX', the biological warfare attack aimed at the western United States, was actually shelved by the Japanese who realized it was a step too far. Would they have been so accommodating if they had known about the American atomic bombs about to be dropped on two of their cities? The war ended just in time to prevent the I-400-class pilots from sallying forth to Ulithi on what would have been one-way missions for all of them.

Fujita's plan cast a long shadow over Japanese submarine operations, but in the end, although the technology was created in time to have made his plan an infinitely more serious proposition than his actual twin attacks in September 1942, circumstances intervened and have left us instead with a series of 'what if' scenarios which the American public fortunately never had to face on their own home ground.

Notes
1. *'Sunk By Submarine, 1944,'* EyeWitness to History, http://www.eyewitnesstohistory.com
2. ibid.
3. ibid.
4. ibid.
5. ibid.
6. Henry Sakaida, Gary Nila & Koji Takaki, *I-400: Japan's Secret Panama Canal Strike Submarine*, (Hikoki Publications), 2006
7. Data derived from Bob Hackett & Sander Kingsepp's *'Sensuikan'*, http://www.combinedfleet.com/sensuikan.htm
8. *The Transpacific Voyage of H.I.J.M.S. I-400*, Tom Paine's Journal: July 1945 to January 1946, (Submarine Warfare Library), 1991
9. ibid.
10. Data derived from Bob Sackett & Sander Kingsepp's *'Sensuikan'*, http://www.combinedfleet.com/type_am.htm
11. Carriers USS *Essex, Intrepid, Wasp, Hancock, Hornet, Belleau Wood* and *Bennington*
12. Data derived from Bob Sackett & Sander Kingsepp's *'Sensuikan'*, http://www.combinedfleet.com/I-13.htm

Appendix 1

Organization of Japanese Submarine Forces 1941–42

Japanese submarines were divided between several separate fleet commands, with most submarines, including all modern fleet boats, mainly under the control of the Sixth Fleet. Older submarines and coastal and transport boats served in several other fleets and forces.

Sixth Fleet (Vice-Admiral Mitsumi Shimizu)
  1st Submarine Squadron (Rear-Admiral Tsutomu Sato)
  2nd Submarine Squadron (Rear-Admiral Shigeteru Yamazaki)
  3rd Submarine Squadron (Rear-Admiral Shigeyoshi Miwa)

The initial tasks of the three squadrons constituting the Sixth Fleet during December 1941 into early 1942 were to destroy the US Pacific Fleet and interdict shipping along the US west coast.

Combined Fleet Headquarters
– 4th Submarine Squadron
– 5th Submarine Squadron (Rear-Admiral Yoshitomi Etuzo)

Combined Fleet HQ retained two squadrons of submarines under its direct command. The flotilla was tasked with destroying Allied surface ships in southern waters and in supporting the Japanese invasions of the Philippines and British Malaya.

Third Fleet (Blockade and Transport)
– 6th Submarine Squadron (Rear-Admiral Chimaki Kono)

The attached submarine squadron was tasked with providing additional naval support during the Japanese landings in the

190

Philippines, Netherlands East Indies and British Malaya, as well as minelaying operations.

Fourth Fleet
– 7th Submarine Squadron (Rear-Admiral Shinzo Onishi)

This squadron, operating older submarines no longer suitable for far-ranging operations, assisted in the protection of both Japanese home waters and mandated Pacific islands.

Kure Naval District Force
– Assorted older submarines

The Force assisted the 7th Squadron in homeland defence and conducted submarine training.

Appendix 2

The Japanese Balloon Bomb Campaign against the United States

The Japanese High Command acknowledged that although the Fujita Plan's overall objective was sound, and both floatplane sorties made by Chief Warrant Officer Fujita had led to the successful delivery of munitions to the United States mainland, the results were negligible. A massive effort was required to transport one very small aircraft across the Pacific onboard a valuable submarine, to drop a tiny amount of bombs onto no specific target. At best it would have proved a propaganda coup had the United States authorities realized that Japan had successfully attacked the American mainland, but very little media coverage emerged. Another munitions delivery system was required, and this time the Japanese decided upon an unmanned and ultra-cheap option: the paper balloon.

Once again, the Japanese required the initial utilization of their submarine force to attack the United States, and in 1943 200 balloons were prepared, and designed to be launched from two modified submarines, the *I-34* and *I-35*. Each balloon had a twenty-foot envelope, and a range of more than 600 miles. Although the operation was fully prepared by August 1943, the Imperial Navy realized that employing submarines on such missions would not have been a sensible use of their potential, especially as the war had long since begun to deteriorate for Japan. The project was shelved, and the navy dropped balloon bomb research. The Imperial Japanese Army, however, continued development instead. The army lacked the means to launch balloons from a mid-point between Japan and the United States, so the new weapons had to be designed to depart from the Japanese homeland itself.

The army balloon-bomb project was codenamed 'Fugo' (Windship Weapon), and the army designers at the 9th Military Technical Research Institute under Major General Sueyoshi Kusaba, in cooperation with scientists of the Central Meteorological Observatory in Tokyo, produced a balloon design that they designated the Type-A (not to be confused with the navy's Type-A midget submarine), made of sixty-four laminated mulberry tree paper gores (the sections forming the curved surface of the balloon). This was glued together with a form of potato paste forming a balloon envelope with a 100-foot circumference. The envelope was then filled with 19,000 cubic feet of hydrogen to provide the necessary high ceiling the weapon required. Below the envelope was suspended a woven dural ring with the bombs and thirty-six ballast sandbags attached, controlled by three aneroid barometers and a C (small) battery mounted on a platform above which controlled a circuit to maintain altitude, and release the bombs. Each balloon carried a payload of two 11-pound thermalite incendiary bombs, and one 33-pound anti-personnel fragmentation bomb. The Japanese called the new weapon *fusen bakudan* or fire bombs. Launch sites were located on the east coast of the main Japanese island of Honshu, at Otsu, Ichinomiryu and Nakaso.

Once released, the balloons were uncontrollable, and carried to the North American continent at the behest of high altitude wind currents, cruising in the jet stream at around 20–40,000 feet. To maintain altitude, sand was automatically released from the ballast bags if the balloon began to sink. In the daytime the balloon would cruise at its maximum altitude, but at night the envelope would collect dew and sink as it became progressively heavier. The altimeter would cause a set of blow plugs to fire, releasing some of the sandbag ballast, thereby restoring the balloon's altitude. When all the sand was gone the bombs would become the final ballast, and they were released automatically – an event calculated to occur over the mainland of the United States. Finally, a picric acid block would explode, destroying the balloon gondola; with a fuse being lit that was connected to a charge on the balloon itself. The resultant mixture of hydrogen, air and explosives would cause the balloon envelope to burn up as a large orange fireball. The balloons were extremely difficult to spot from the ground, because they cruised at such a high altitude, and most American fighter aircraft of the period could not reach them.

The first balloon launch occurred on 3 November 1944, with a US Navy patrol boat discovering a balloon floating in the sea sixty-six miles off San Pedro, California on 5 November. The first known successful attack on the United States occurred on 6 December 1944, bombs being dropped around twelve miles south-west of Owl Creek Mountain, close to Thermopolis, Wyoming. Fragments of balloon envelopes and gondolas were discovered in Alaska and Montana, and forensic tests confirmed the wreckage to be of Japanese origin. The question was how were the Japanese delivering the weapons to the United States?

The people of the United States were not informed of the attacks, and the media was ordered not to report this alarming development. The United States also developed counter-measures to deal with this unique threat, codenamed 'Operation Firefly.' The US 4th Air Force gathered fighter squadrons to shoot down the balloons before they could release their payloads, and many were downed over the Aleutian Islands before they could reach their targets as they sank to lower altitudes. One was shot down over Oregon. There was a fear among the American authorities that the Japanese could have used the balloons to deliver chemical and biological warfare agents to the United States, and to counter any such threat stocks of decontamination chemicals were quietly distributed to the western states, and farmers were asked to report any strange crop markings or animal infections that occurred. Although the United States authorities played down the potential damage that balloon bombs could have wreaked, Lyle Watts of the Agricultural Department commenting in June 1945 that, '...the forest service was "less worried about this Japanese balloon attack than we are with matches and smokes in the hands of good Americans hiking and camping in the woods".' A US Army unit, 555th Parachute Infantry Battalion (nicknamed the 'Triple Nickle' because of their unit number) was trained to act as fire jumpers should the incendiary bombs set the forests ablaze.

Of the 9,300 balloons launched from Japan, only 212 were

confirmed as having arrived in the United States and Mexico, landing as far east in the United States as Michigan, and a further seventy-three were confirmed as coming down in Canada. The only fatalities caused by the balloon bombs occurred on 5 May 1945, on Gearhart Mountain, near Bly, Oregon. A picnicking party of one adult and five children were tragically killed instantly when they dragged an unexploded Imperial Japanese Navy 15-kg anti-personnel bomb out of the woods. These six people are the only known fatalities caused by enemy action on mainland United States during the Second World War. It is not known whether any of the balloon bombs started forest fires, as was intended.

In April 1945, the Japanese ceased their balloon launches, largely because of the American media blackout that had told them nothing about the success or failure of the campaign. What remains certain, however, is the fact that many of the bombs remain unaccounted for, and after over sixty years of deterioration could pose a serious risk to anyone who discovered one of these strange relics in the American countryside today.

Appendix 3

A Japanese Landing in Australia

For all the panic among the civilian population of Australia concerning a Japanese invasion in mid-1942, the Japanese never intended to carry out such an operation. Only on one occasion late in the war did Japanese troops come ashore in Australia.

By January 1944 Japanese naval intelligence suspected that the United States was constructing a new naval base at Admiralty Gulf on the north-western shores of Western Australia. The navy made a request to the closest military forces to Western Australia to conduct a reconnaissance to confirm or deny their suspicions. Based on Ambon Island, the Japanese 19th Army contained a special commando-style unit called the *Matsu Kikan*, or Pine Tree, under the command of Captain Masayoshi Yamamoto. The *Matsu Kikan* contained graduates of the Army Intelligence School at Nakano in Japan, and they formed an elite reconnaissance force. Captain Yamamoto detailed one of his subordinates, Lieutenant Susuhiko Mizuno, to put together a small team ready for insertion into Western Australia. Mizuno's tasks were threefold: firstly, he was to investigate the possibility of effecting a landing in Australia, secondly, find a good location where a force could be put ashore, and thirdly, scout around and try to find any military establishments in the region.

Lieutenant Mizuno's party departed on their mission from Koepang in Timor (part of the Japanese occupied Netherlands East Indies) aboard a tiny 25-ton fishing vessel called the *Hiroshi Maru* on 14 January 1944. The rest of Mizuno's team consisted of two sergeants, a superior private who would act as a radio operator, six Japanese sailors, and fifteen local Timorese disguised as fishermen. The Timorese would sail the vessel to Australia, and if any Allied aircraft or ships encountered the *Hiroshi Maru* their presence would hopefully deter a more thorough investigation of the boat. The first attempt to conduct the mission was a failure, however, as the tiny fishing boat was caught in a ferocious storm that forced Mizuno to scrub the operation and return to base on the morning of 15 January.

The Japanese waited the storm out and then departed again on the evening of 16 January. Strangely, although the Japanese had already disguised their activities with the addition of the Timorese, they now took the contradictory step of providing the *Hiroshi Maru* with air cover for the voyage. Any Allied plane or ship that encountered a small fishing boat with its own dedicated aerial cover would arouse suspicion. 19th Army Headquarters instructed the 7th Air Division at Kendari to release an aircraft for the operation, and Staff Sergeant Aonuma found himself flying his Type 99 light bomber on circuits around the *Hiroshi Maru* as she motored towards Australia.

On 16 January, as the fishing boat approached Cartier Islet, Aonuma spotted a submarine running on the surface. Undoubtedly Allied, Aonuma decided to dissuade the submarine from making a close inspection of the *Hiroshi Maru*, and dived in to attack. Lookouts aboard the submarine had already spotted the Japanese aircraft, and the submarine immediately crash-dived, followed under the waves by two bursts of machine-gun fire from the Type 99. As Aonuma passed over the white water, marking where the submarine had vanished, he dropped six 50kg bombs. The bombs detonated underwater, and Aonuma circled over the spot several times, later reporting that the submarine had probably been damaged.

The Type 99 light bomber continued her mission of flying cover for the *Hiroshi Maru* as the vessel approached the Australian coast. A radar system monitored the airspace over the coastline, forcing the Japanese aircraft to drop down low. Flying ahead of the fishing boat, Aonuma located Cartier Islet, returning to guide the *Hiroshi Maru* in. The first 'landfall' made by the Japanese was at 9 a.m. on 17 January, when they reached East Island. The island is actually a coral reef that is exposed during low tide. Twenty-four hours later the Japanese reached Browse Island, and here Lieutenant Mizuno and his men went ashore. Browse contained nothing except a ruined watchtower, but the island did provide the Japanese force with a suitable laying-up position. Timing his mission carefully, Mizuno wanted the force to land on the mainland in the early morning of 19 January. After three hours on Browse, the *Hiroshi Maru* weighed anchor and sailed through the night to the mainland, entering an inlet on the coast of Western Australia at approximately 10 a.m., the first Japanese troops to land in Australia.

A light mist concealed the Japanese landing party as they quietly collected tree branches with which to camouflage the *Hiroshi Maru*, then the men ate a cold breakfast before beginning their mission. Mizuno now divided his command into three parties tasked with exploring different areas of the wilderness. Mizuno commanded one, while the two sergeants, Morita and Furuhashi, each led another, and it was agreed that all parties would rendezvous back at the boat after two hours. Mizuno even had a 8mm movie camera with him to record anything of interest that was discovered.

The Japanese were to discover nothing of any military interest, all parties reporting only finding old campfires. After a night aboard the boat Mizuno ordered another series of patrols on 20 January, but by 2 p.m., and with nothing to show for their labours, Mizuno decided to end the mission and return to Timor. The Japanese landings near Cartier and Browse Islands in Western Australia remain the only confirmed presence of enemy troops in Australia during the Second World War, though many locals and amateur historians insist that Japanese reconnaissance parties undertook several similar missions to Australia, and that Japanese submarine crews also came ashore in quiet localities for fresh water.

Appendix 4

German U-boat operations around Australia

A single German U-boat, *U-862*, ventured into the Pacific Ocean and around the coast of Australia to interdict Allied shipping during the Second World War. Indeed, the commander of *U-862*, Lieutenant-Commander Heinrich Timm, possessed a special record when Germany surrendered in May 1945. He was the only U-boat skipper to have conducted war patrols in the Atlantic, Indian and Pacific Oceans. From 1943 German submarines were based at a series of ports throughout south-east Asia, as part of an agreement between Germany and Japan. The German U-boat bases were located at Penang off Malaya, Surabaya in Java, Singapore, Batavia in the Netherlands East Indies and at the Japanese port of Kobe. Their role was two-fold, with about half conducting offensive operations into the Indian Ocean and around southern Africa, and the rest, assisted by some obsolescent Italian submarines, delivering secret cargoes of weapons and raw materials between German-occupied Europe and the Japanese sphere of operations. This was codenamed the Yanagi trade, and was of high priority to both Axis partners.

On 3 June 1944, *U-862* had departed from Norway headed for the German U-boat base at Batavia. As was usual, *U-862* would conduct a war patrol on the journey to the Far East, and Timm scored some successes. He attacked and sank the 6,885-ton United States ship *Robin Goodfellow* on 25 July in the South Atlantic. In the Indian Ocean, *U-862* scored a second kill, sinking the 3,614-ton *Radbury* on 13 August while the U-boat was to the south of the island of Madagascar. Timm's successes continued as his boat sailed across the Indian Ocean towards its new Far Eastern base, and on 16 August *U-862* sank the 7,037-ton *Empire Lancer*. Two days later *U-862* struck again, sinking the 5,414-ton *Nairung*. Success followed success, and on 19 August he made a successful attack on the 5,068-ton British ship *Wayfarer*. On *U-862*'s arrival at Batavia on 17 September 1944 Timm was awarded the Knights Cross, Nazi Germany's pre-eminent decoration for gallantry and meritorious service. However, Timm's run of successes was not without incident. On 20 August, *U-862* was in the northern section of the Mozambique Channel, beginning to nose into the Indian Ocean proper, when a Catalina anti-submarine aircraft of the RAF's 265 Squadron, which was engaged on a transport flight from Mombasa to Durban, caught the U-boat on the surface. The Catalina was carrying an additional four RAF maintenance crew as passengers alongside the normal four aircrew complement of the aircraft, but the pilot was conducting anti-submarine surveillance on route to South Africa. As the aircraft swung in to attack the U-boat firing its nose gun, the submarine's 37mm flak gun returned fire, scoring hits on the aircraft's starboard engine and wing. As the aircraft closed the distance between itself and the U-boat, the 20mm flak gunners aboard *U-862* pumped several rounds into the cockpit, which presumably killed or incapacitated the pilot. The Catalina crashed into the sea a mere thirty feet beyond the U-boat, leaving no survivors. *U-862* emerged from the battle without so much as a scratch on her paintwork.[1]

On 17 November 1944, *U-862* set out from Batavia harbour on a war patrol designed to take the lone German submarine into the waters off Australia, which Timm had plied before the war while a merchant navy officer. *U-862* sailed down the west coast of Australia, and then turned east. On 9 December, in broad daylight, the surfaced *U-862* bombarded the 4,724-ton Greek tanker *Ilissos* with her 105mm deck-gun, and managed to inflict some damage. However, the tanker had aboard her a small party of armed guards manning a 4-inch gun, and with this the tanker was able to return the German's fire. Rather than risk any damage to his submarine while so far from proper repair facilities Timm submerged *U-862*. With the report of an enemy submarine, probably German, operating just off the Australian coast, the

RAAF scrambled a fleet of aircraft to begin a search for the intruder. The Royal Australian Navy's corvettes HMAS *Lismore, Burnie* and *Maryborough* conducted sweeps through the area in which Timm had attacked the *Ilissos*. Timm was unaware of the hunt then underway for his U-boat and went on to make another kill on Christmas Eve 1944, when he sank the 7,180-ton American Liberty ship *Robert J Walker* off Montague Island, New South Wales. Timm's final kill of the patrol was another American Liberty ship, the 7,176-ton *Peter Silvester*, loaded with US Army supplies and 137 army mules, which he sank off the Australian west coast as Timm took *U-862* back to Batavia on 6 February 1945. Only fifteen survivors from the *Peter Silvester* were plucked from the ocean on 9 February. Liberator aircraft of No. 25 Squadron, RAAF, located another fifty survivors drifting on life rafts on 12 and 13 February, and dropped rations to the survivors. The last survivors of the sinking of the *Peter Silvester* were not located and rescued by the American submarine USS *Rock* until 9 March.

On 27 February 1945 *U-862* arrived in Japanese-occupied Singapore. While at Singapore the combined 37mm and 20mm flak gunners aboard the U-boat successfully shot down a USAAF P-38 Lightning fighter-bomber during an air raid on the port in early May 1945.[2]

On 3 May, Captain Kurt Freiwald, the skipper of *U-181*, another U-boat based in the port, addressed all German servicemen who were in Singapore, and informed them that Hitler had died in Berlin. Thereafter the Japanese interned the Germans until their own final surrender on 15 August 1945, and the Imperial Navy seized all the remaining U-boats.

Notes
1. N. Franks and E. Zimmerman, *U-Boat versus Aircraft*, (London: Grub Street), 1998, p.167
2. ibid., p.184

Sources and Bibliography

Archives

National Archives of Australia, Canberra

1. Midget submarine attack on Sydney Harbour – MP1049/5, 2026/21/79
2. (Japanese) Midget Submarine Attack on Sydney Harbour, 31May/1 June 1942 – SP338/1 201/37
3. Midget Submarine Attack on Sydney Harbour – Signals – B6121/162K

Australian War Memorial, Canberra

1. Japanese midget submarine attack on Sydney Harbour, night of 31 May/1June 1942. Reconstruction of events from Japanese and Australian Sources by G. Hermon Gill – AWM54/622/5/8

National Archives and Records Administration (NARA), Washington, DC.

1. Film Nix/DK
a. Commanding Officer to Commander in Chief, US Asiatic Fleet, Action taken against Submarines by USS *Edsall*, 31 January 1942
b. Confidential Action Report. Activities of USS *Edsall* for 20-31 January [Covers anti-submarine operations while escorting 'Trinity' to Port Darwin, Australia], 22 January 1942
c. Commander Destroyer Squadron Twenty-Nine to The Commander, US Naval Forces Southwest Pacific, 1st Endorsement on CO *EDSALL*, 10 February 1942

Published Sources

Bagnasco, E., *Submarines of World War Two*, (Annapolis: Naval Institute Press), 1977

Boyd, Carl & Yoshida, Akira, *The Japanese Submarine Force and World War II*, (Shrewsbury: Airlife Publishing Ltd), 1996

Cook, Haruko Taya and Cook, Theodore F., *Japan at War: An Oral History*, (New Press), 1993

Dull, Paul, *A Battle History of the Imperial Japanese Navy, 1941–45*, (Annapolis: Naval Institute Press), 1978

Elliot, P., *Allied Escort Ships of World War II*, (Annapolis: Naval Institute Press), 1977

Felton, Mark, *Yanagi: The Secret Underwater Trade between Germany and Japan, 1942–1945*, (Barnsley: Pen & Sword Maritime), 2005

Gill, G. Hermon, *Royal Australian Navy, 1941–1942*, (Canberra: Australian War Memorial), 1968

Goldstein, Donald M., *At Dawn We Slept: The Untold Story of Pearl Harbor (Revised Edition)*, (London: Penguin), 1991

Goldstein, Donald M. (Editor) and Dillon, Katherine (Editor), *The Pearl Harbor Papers: Inside the Japanese Plans*, (New York: Potomac Books), 1999

Hashimoto, M., *Sunk: The Story of the Japanese Submarine Fleet, 1941–1945*, (New York: Henry Holt & Co.), 1954

Herman, Arthur, *To Rule the Waves: How the British Navy Shaped the Modern World*, (London: Hodder & Stoughton), 2005

Horn, Steve, *The Second Attack on Pearl Harbor: Operation K and Other Japanese Attempts to Bomb America in World War II*, (Annapolis: Naval Institute Press), 2005

Ito, Masanori with Kuroda, Andrew and Pineau, Roger (translators), *The End of the Imperial Japanese Navy*, (Greenwood Press), 1984

Japanese Monograph No. 97, Pearl Harbor Operations: General Outline of Orders and Plans, (Washington D.C.: Office of the Chief of Military History, Department of the Army), 1953

Jenkins, David, *Battle Surface! Japan's Submarine War against Australia, 1942–44*, (London: Random House), 1992

Jentschura, Hansgeorg, Jung, Dieter and Michel, Peter, *Warships of the Imperial Japanese Navy, 1869–1945*, (Annapolis: Naval Institute Press), 1976

Kemp, Paul, *Underwater Warriors: The Fighting History of Midget Submarines*, (London: Cassell Military Paperbacks), 2001

Miller, David, *U-Boats: History, Development and Equipment 1914–1945*, (London: Conway Maritime Press), 2000

Milligan, Christopher S. and Foley, John C.H., *Australian Hospital Ship Centaur: The Myth of Immunity,* (Hendra: Nairana Publications), 1993

Mollo, Andrew, *The Armed Forces of World War II,* (London: MacDonald & Co. (Publishers) Ltd.), 1981

Paine, Tom, *The Transpacific Voyage of H.I.J.M.S. I-400,* Tom Paine's Journal: July 1945 to January 1946, (Submarine Warfare Library), 1991

Polmar, Norman & Carpenter, Dorr B., *Submarines of the Imperial Japanese Navy 1904–1945,* (London: Conway Maritime Press), 1986

Prange, Gordon W. with Goldstein, Donald M., and Dillon, Katherine V., *Dec. 7 1941: The Day Japan Attacked Pearl Harbor,* (London: Harrap Limited), 1988

Report of the Joint Committee on the Investigation of the Pearl Harbor attack, Congress of the United States, (Washington D.C.: Government Printing Office), 1946

Rohwer, J., *Axis Submarine Successes, 1939–1945,* (Annapolis: Naval Institute Press), 1983

Russell, Lord, of Liverpool, *The Knights of Bushido: A Short History of Japanese War Crimes,* (London: Greenhill Books), 2002

Sakaida, Henry, Nila, Gary & Takaki, Koji, *I-400: Japan's Secret Panama Canal Strike Submarine,* (Hikoki Publications), 2006

Smith, Colin, *Singapore Burning: Heroism and Surrender in World War II,* (London: Viking), 2005

Spector, R., *Eagle Against the Sun,* (New York: Free Press/MacMillan), 1985

Thomas, David A., *Japan's War At Sea: Pearl Harbor to the Coral Sea,* (London: Andre Deutsch), 1978

Warner, Peggy & Seno, Sadao, *The Coffin Boats: Japanese Midget Submarine Operations in the Second World War,* (London: Secker & Warburg Ltd), 1986

Webber, Burt, *Silent Siege: Japanese Attacks against North America in World War II,* (Fairfield: Ye Galleon), 1984

Silent Siege III: Japanese Attacks on North America in World War II, (Medford: Webb Research Group), 1992

Newspapers and Journals

Aviation History
Edmonton Journal
Journal of the Australian War Memorial
Newcastle Morning Herald

New York Times
Proceedings
Sydney Morning Herald
World War II

Speeches

The Hon. Danna Vale MP, Minister for Veterans' Affairs, Minister Assisting the Minister for Defence, at the Fort Scratchley Dedication Dinner at City Hall, Newcastle, 2002

Address by His Excellency Major General Michael Jeffrey AC, MVO, MC, Governor-General of the Commonwealth of Australia on the occasion of Warringah Australia Remembers Trust Commemorative Service to mark the 62nd anniversary of the defence of Sydney: Manly, New South Wales, 28 May 2004

Websites

California State Military Museum, http://www.militarymuseum.org
Commonwealth Department of Veterans' Affairs, Australia, http://www.dva.gov.au
Eyewitness to History, http://www.eyewitnesstohistory.com
Historynet website, http://www.historynet.com
Sensuikan! (Bob Hackett & Sander Kingsepp), http://www.combinedfleet.com

Index

206

208